WRITERS CONFERENCE
AT PENN

WRITERS CONFERENCE AT PENN

October 14-15, 2006

University of Pennsylvania

To order additional copies of this book, contact:
Xlibris Corporation
1-888-795-4274
www.Xlibris.com
Orders@Xlibris.com
35369

CONTENTS

INTRODUCTION

Dear Writers Conference Attendee,

More than a year of planning goes into organizing the Writers Conference at Penn to ensure a range of topics and instructors with a wide appeal in fiction and nonfiction can be offered. Our aim is to provide value in the form of workshops about the craft of writing, the pleasure of writing, the value of writing, as well as representations of the various ways writers can ply their trade.

We make a dedicated effort to ensure that this conference is a forum for sharing your ideas with other writers in a thought provoking, constructive format. Past participants comment that this conference gives them inspiration and motivation as well as teaching them valuable skills.

Special Workshop Book

For this, our 12th Writers Conference at Penn, we are pleased to offer you a volume of materials and work from the workshop leaders. This book is an effort made possible by the support of our conference instructors and Xlibris, an on-demand publishing services provider located here in Philadelphia.

Many previous conference attendees have mentioned how difficult it is to choose among our numerous workshops and have asked to learn more about the workshops or instructors they missed. This book is an eclectic mix of workshop materials and excerpts from the instructors' own work, arranged alphabetically by instructor.

We truly hope you enjoy this conference. If you have been with us in the past, thank you for joining us again and if this is new to you, we look forward to meeting and exceeding your expectations.

Please make sure to visit us throughout the year as we offer a host of excellent writing classes taught by many of the instructors you will meet today. Our website is *www.pennclasses.org* and our phone number is 215-898-6493.

Thank you again for your participation and support.

Sincerely,
The Writers Conference at Penn

AN INVITATION . . .

The Penn Bookstore is pleased to partner once again with the Annual Writers Conference at Penn.

All attendees of the conference are invited to attend a cocktail reception and book signing at the Penn Bookstore on Saturday, October 14th from 6:00-8:00pm. All attendees will receive a 20% discount on books purchased that weekend.

The Penn Bookstore, situated in the heart of University Square, functions as both a collegiate bookstore and a full-service Barnes and Noble superstore. Of its 130,000 titles, 90,000 are academic books, making it one of the most comprehensive academic bookstores in the nation.

The 50,000 square foot Bookstore features a Faculty Authors area as well as an extensive children's book section. A 100-seat café offers a pleasant venue to drink coffee or eat a snack. In addition to books and supplies, the Penn Bookstore includes a comprehensive music and DVD department with listening boards; a poster and print department; and a vast assortment of clothing and gifts sporting the Penn insignia.

The Penn Bookstore coordinates a full schedule of readings by authors, many of them Penn faculty or alumni.

A SPECIAL THANK YOU TO OUR PARTNERS:

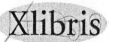

SUSAN Q. STRANAHAN

KEYNOTE SPEAKER

SUSAN Q. STRANAHAN

Keynote speaker Biography

Susan Q. Stranahan is the director of communications at the Annenberg Public Policy Center of the University of Pennsylvania. She is the author of *Susquehanna River of Dreams*, a natural history of the Susquehanna River, published in 1993 by The Johns Hopkins University Press. (The book recently was issued in its third printing.)

For 28 years, she was a staff member at The Philadelphia Inquirer, serving as a reporter, editor and member of the Inquirer's editorial board. During that time she wrote extensively on regional and national environmental issues. In 1979, she wrote many of the news stories about the Three Mile Island nuclear accident for which The Inquirer was awarded the 1980 Pulitzer Prize for General Local Reporting. She has also been a Pulitzer Prize finalist on two occasions.

In addition, she served as a staff writer for CJR Daily, a website at the Columbia University Graduate School of Journalism that monitors media coverage. She has worked as a freelance journalist whose work has appeared in *Fortune*, *The Washington Post*, *The Los Angeles Times*, *American Journalism Review* and other publications.

MARLENE ARCHIE

CULTURAL PLACES AND LOCATIONS: LITERARY SKETCH AND THE WRITER

Marlene Archie
Cultural Places and Locations: Literary Sketch and the Writer

WORKSHOP DESCRIPTION

A writer's cultural place is recognizable through the examination of language, direction and attitude in texts. Some aspect of your cultural place—where/how you are positioned or located in terms of culture is can be identified for the serious reader who seeks to understand the center of the text, sketch or data under discussion. This creative nonfiction workshop begins with defining culture, discussing location theory, and locating several cultural sketches. Students will bring to the workshop a short narrative (500 words or less) on when "you" became aware that you were a cultural being—when did that happen and how? We will create a time line of the periods of discovery of that knowledge. Workshop members will then work collaboratively to identify the part of their text that supports their determination of where they are located culturally. From the student's literary sketch, which can be an entertaining account of some aspect of their culture, workshop members will explore their own and others' cultural position while developing, through workshop input, their original writing. Students should bring five copies of their narrative.

INSTRUCTOR BIOGRAPHY

Marlene Archie is a member of the English Department at Arcadia University where she teaches diversity themes in English literature courses. Her specialty is Afrocentric literary analysis. She has contributed articles to *A Casebook for Student Writers*, for first year writers at Arcadia, and published academic essays in her area of specialty. She has a PhD in African-American Studies from Temple University.

TANYA MARIA BARRIENTOS

THE FUNNY THING ABOUT HUMOR WRITING

Tanya Maria Barrientos
The Funny Thing About Humor Writing

WORKSHOP DESCRIPTION

You cannot learn how to have a sense of humor, or how to adopt a comic view of the world. But if you have a knack for being funny, you can learn a few key techniques that will help your humor shine on the page. For stand-up comedians it's all in the timing and, in a way, the same rule applies when it comes to humor writing. The difference is for a writer "timing" means something very different because a joke has to work visually instead of verbally. How's that done? That's what this master class will be about, the not-so-funny part of writing nonfiction humor essays. What makes David Sedaris and Steve Martin so good at it? In this class you'll deconstruct their work (and that of others) and learn how to apply their techniques to your own work.

INSTRUCTOR BIOGRAPHY

Tanya Maria Barrientos writes the 'Unconventional Wisdom' column for *The Philadelphia Inquirer*, where she has been a staff writer for twenty years. Author of two novels, *Frontera Street* and *Family Resemblance*, she was awarded the Pew Fellowship of the Arts and has also received a Pennsylvania Council on the Arts Grant.

ROBB BETTIKER

GUNSHOTS, ARSENIC, AND BLEEDING
OUT YOUR EYES: A PHYSICIAN'S VIEW ON
WRITING ABOUT MURDER, POISONS, AND
BIOTERRORISM

Robb Bettiker
Gunshots, Arsenic, and Bleeding Out Your Eyes:
A Physician's View on Writing about Murder, Poisons, and
Bioterrorism

WORKSHOP DESCRIPTION

Are you writing a thriller and wondering, for example, which major disease would be most useful if you wanted to wipe out a city's population? Or, no matter what genre you write in, how do you find medically accurate information when needed? In this workshop, a physician will guide you through an overview of the medical details of mayhem and murder in literature. Topics include the effects of a gunshot or a stabbing on the human body, a quick look at some classic poisons, and a listing and brief description of a selection of those useful major diseases. You'll also learn how to find information in textbooks, on the Internet, and from other sources. Bring your questions and any relevant sections of your work you'd like to discuss.

INSTRUCTOR BIOGRAPHY

Robb Bettiker, M.D., is an attending physician in infectious diseases at Temple University Hospital and is on the faculty of Temple University Medical School. He was previously in private practice in Bryn Mawr and was an adjunct professor of Family Medicine in Bryn Mawr Hospital's residency program. He has written a number of articles and essays, lectured at Temple University Hospital and Bryn Mawr Hospital, and is a candidate for a regional task force on bioterrorism. He holds a B.S. in chemistry from the Massachusetts Institute of Technology, a Masters in Government Administration from the Fels Center of Government at the University of Pennsylvania and a M.D. from Georgetown University. He writes poetry and gardens in his spare time.

ROBIN BLACK

ROMANCING THE DRASTIC

Robin Black
Romancing The Drastic

WORKSHOP DESCRIPTION

What is to be gained by taking the straightforward short story you just wrote, saving that version and then rewriting the whole thing as a series of e-mails between the characters? What might you learn if, just for fun, you then told it again from the perspective of the house in which the action takes place? As writers, many of us struggle with being attached to the particulars of how we first put words on the page. We tend to revise within a set of parameters defined by what we first assumed the story should be. But what possibilities might we discover if while revising our pieces we set no limits on the changes we might make? This class is designed to help free you from some of your attachment to your own first drafts by introducing you to the idea of drastic revision, as a means to better understanding your own work and your own intentions. Each student is invited to submit up to 2,000 words of fiction or nonfiction. All submissions will receive comments from the instructor, and three or four pieces will be worked on in class. This will not be a typical workshop; rather we will be using the student works as jumping off points for exploring how the authors might experiment with drastic changes as part of the process through which they explore and revise their own work. Please make it clear on your manuscript if you prefer not to have your work shared with the class. Manuscripts must be submitted two weeks before the class date. You will be instructed how to submit your manuscript after you register for the workshop.

INSTRUCTOR BIOGRAPHY

Robin Black is a graduate of the Warren Wilson College MFA Program for Writers. Her fiction has appeared or is forthcoming in numerous publications including the *Alaska Quarterly Review*, *Colorado Review*, *Indiana Review* and *The Southern Review*. For the past two years, stories of hers have received Special Mention in the Pushcart Prize Volume. A MacDowell Colony Fellow and recipient of a Leeway Foundation Grant for Emerging Artists, she is also the winner of the 2005 Pirates Alley Faulkner/Wisdom Writing Competition in the short story category. Robin spent several years as a member of Rittenhouse Writers Group and has taught at Arcadia University as well as the Penn Writers Conference.

BERTIE BREGMAN
&
CRAIG A. IRVINE

STORIES IN MEDICINE:
WRITING ABOUT ILLNESS AND HEALING

Bertie Bregman & Craig A. Irvine
Stories in Medicine: Writing About Illness And Healing.

WORKSHOP DESCRIPTION

Illness touches us all, whether as patients, family, or clinicians, and many have been drawn to writing as a way of processing their encounters with the medical world. This workshop is for those who would like to write about their experiences with illness and disease, treatments and procedures, doctors and medicine. We will begin by reviewing the rationale for a narrative approach to medicine. We will then lead participants through sessions that include the reading and writing of poetry and/or prose. Everyone will have the opportunity to share his or her work with other participants and receive feedback in a supportive, respectful atmosphere.

INSTRUCTOR BIOGRAPHY

Bertie Bregman, M.D., is chief of hospital services for family medicine at the Columbia University Medical Center in New York and a faculty member in the Program for Narrative Medicine at the University's College of Physicians and Surgeons. Over the past five years, he has designed innovative Medical Humanities and Narrative Medicine curricula for medical students, residents and faculty. His articles and reviews have appeared in Family Medicine, The Lancet, and other journals. He has presented these curricula in seminars and workshops at numerous national conferences. He received his M.D. degree from the University of Pennsylvania School of Medicine.

Craig A. Irvine, PhD., is Director of Education for the Program in Narrative Medicine and Research Administrator in the Center For Family Medicine at Columbia University College of Physicians and Surgeons. He has over twenty years of experience teaching ethics and humanities. For the past six years, he has been designing and teaching cultural competency, ethics, Narrative Medicine, and Humanities and Medicine curricula for residents, medical students and faculty. He holds a doctorate in Philosophy from Pennsylvania State University.

MEREDITH BROUSSARD

MYTHOLOGIZING THE MUNDANE: HOW TO WRITE ABOUT EVERYDAY LIFE

Meredith Broussard
Mythologizing the Mundane: How To Write About
Everyday Life

WORKSHOP DESCRIPTION

Have you ever read a column or personal essay, and wondered how
the author made ordinary events seem remarkable? Have you ever
experienced something unusual, and wondered how to write about it?
Does your imagination run wild when you're bored? Do you make up
stories about people you see in restaurants, or "accidentally" listen to
the conversation at the next table over? If so, join us for a discussion
of how to turn ordinary life into literature. You'll draw on your powers
of imagination and observation, and complete a series of exercises to
help you write compelling fiction and creative nonfiction about life
as you know it. We'll discuss the difference between "plot" and "a
series of events," and talk about the ethics of writing about people
you know. We'll also look at writers like Joan Didion, Calvin Trillin,
and Jonathan Franzen, and talk about how writers can make ordinary
life seem transcendent.

INSTRUCTOR BIOGRAPHY

Meredith Broussard is a writer, critic and editor of an anthology, *The
Dictionary of Failed Relationships: 26 Stories of Love Gone Wrong* (Three
Rivers Press, 2003), and *the Encyclopedia of Exes: 26 Stories by Men of
Love Gone Wrong* (Three Rivers Press, 2005). Her stories and reviews
have appeared in a variety of publications, including *Philadelphia
Magazine, The Philadelphia Inquirer, The San Francisco Chronicle, The
Chicago Reader,* and *The New York Press.* She is one of the original
organizers of Philadelphia's 215 Festival of Books and Music, and is
a member of the National Book Critics' Circle and the Pennsylvania

Association of Black Journalists, a graduate of Harvard University, and holds an MFA in creative writing from Columbia University. As of April, she is also the proud mother of Nathaniel Scott. Her Web site is *www.failedrelationships.com.*

PHIL CAMPBELL

MEMOIR WRITING IS NOT BLOGGING

SUPPLEMENTARY MATERIALS:

EXCERPT: *ZIONCHECK FOR PRESIDENT:*
A TRUE STORY OF IDEALISM AND
MADNESS IN AMERICAN POLITICS

Phil Campbell
Memoir Writing Is Not Blogging

WORKSHOP DESCRIPTION

Memoir writing is not blogging. Nor is it self-therapy. In fact, in a world where everyone is told they "have a book in them," personal writing is one of the most difficult forms to master, precisely because it sounds so easy. In this class we will tackle this art form head-on-by exploring the memoirs that ignore all the rules and turn the genre on its head. We will study memoirs that use great writing, intriguing structure, or unique themes to wrest the story away from the individual to move toward something larger (like Joan Didion's *The Year of Magical Thinking* and James Ellroy's *My Dark Places*), as well as the books that take something unrelated and tie it implicitly to the writer (like Susan Orlean's *The Orchid Thief* and Jonathan Raban's *A Passage to Juneau*). Please come with a sense of humor, a desire to participate, and the expectation that Jessica Cutler, Mary Cheney, and James Frey will, inevitably, be ridiculed.

INSTRUCTOR BIOGRAPHY

Phil Campbell's first published work of non-fiction appeared in Dave Eggers' *Might Magazine*, about the time he persuaded 22 other Phil Campbells and one Phyllis Campbell to join him for a convention in the town of Phil Campbell, Alabama (the event also earned him a mention in *Ripleys—Believe it or Not!*). He worked for six years as a reporter for alternative weeklies, and most recently authored *Zioncheck for President: A True Story of Idealism and Madness in American Politics*, an eccentric memoir about his experiences with lefty campaign politics in Seattle, Washington.

An excerpt from Phillip Campbell's
Zioncheck for President: A True Story of Idealism and Madness in American Politics

A noise startled me. Doug towered over me at the edge of the couch, a loaded Corona in his right hand, a lime slice balanced on the top of its neck. I really should have stayed in my room.

"Hi Doug," I said, greeting my housemate with a mixture of suspicion and dread.

Doug squeezed the lime slice into his bottle with his right fist and watched its juices mix with the alcohol. He took a swig and stared at me expectantly. Doug had a doughy, six-foot-three-inch body and a thick red mustache, which he licked from time to time with his tongue. He looked like a walrus whose territory was constantly threatened by smaller animals.

"Oh, hey, Phil," he said. "Did Emily tell you about her problem? There's a smell of raw sewage every morning in her bathroom. She gets it every time someone flushes the upstairs toilet." His sentences were soaked with overly polite, calculated pauses.

"Yes," I said. "We've been talking about it for more than a week now. I told her that I was on it."

"Well, if you need any help, just let me know. I went down there but didn't smell anything. I guess it only happens in the morning, when we flush the toilet upstairs."

I averted my eyes and looked out one of the far windows in the dining area. It was so smudged with dirt that I could barely see the hawthorn tree outside. Six months before, Doug had gathered up the courage to tell me that he could manage the house better than I could. Though caught off guard, I had rebuffed him, knowing that what he was really after was my rent discount. My mind hadn't changed.

"Yes, I guess you're right," I said.

"Oh, and the lawn—" he said.

"*Yes*. You're probably right."

"—you think you're going to mow it any time soon? It probably needs it."

"Yes. You—are—probably—*right*."

Doug stared at me for a moment while his fat fingers reached for a cigarette pack and plastic lighter in his denim jacket pocket. He made a sniffling sound and headed for the porch.

Through the front window, I could see Doug engaging in his usual smoking ritual. He played with the cigarette for a while, at one point sticking it behind his ear in the way an absent-minded desk clerk might store a pencil. Then he grabbed it back and lit it, taking desultory puffs. He stared out at traffic, oblivious to everything but the motion of the cars. He did not move for a long time.

A small, wild impulse seized me. Doug and I used to get along really well. I headed outside.

On seeing me, my housemate stirred slightly and flicked cigarette ash over the porch railing. He was peeved, I could tell, but did his best to mask it.

"What's up?" he said.

"Oh. Uh, nothing, I guess." I plopped down on the wicker couch that pressed against the house. "My life blows chunks."

He didn't seem to hear me or want to hear me, and I was forced to stare at traffic with him.

Front porches in Seattle are an anomaly. Backyard decks and patios were preferred, perhaps because there the guest list could be restricted. The few front stoops in the city were generally used for other, nonsocial purposes, like daydreaming or drinking or smoking alone. Doug was well suited for these activities, and he used the porch more than the rest of us. He roamed its gray cement as if searching for trespassers. Doug was from some small town in rural Washington—I could never remember which—and this made me think he would never be at home in a city.

"That was a really great party the other weekend, wasn't it?" he finally said, his eyes on some distant point down the block.

"Yeah, it was. Hey, where were you? I didn't see you after like nine o'clock."

"Upstairs. With my brother."

"Oh." So Doug had disappeared into his room to drink with only one other person. This was odd because he had contributed more money for the party than the rest of us.

The cars moved through the lights of Twenty-third Avenue like ships plying a river canal.

"The cops came three times," I said.

This seemed to rouse him. "Really? Awesome!"

"You didn't see them?" Of course he hadn't.

"Yeah," I said, warming up to it. "Three *times*. The last time they were so mad they threatened to confiscate all the DJ's equipment."

"What the hell? Why?"

"Neighbor complaints. It was only eleven-thirty!"

"Fucking neighbors. Can't handle a little old party on a Saturday night."

"I guess it was because all the smokers were hanging out on the porch, and they couldn't deal with that," I said. "And the thing was, we had a city councilmember here. God, I totally didn't think of it. I should have sent him out there to talk to them! I wonder how they would have acted."

"Awwwwww," Doug marveled. "And we didn't even use my speakers. Those damn things would have woken up all of Bellevue!" Bellevue was the suburb to the east. Doug had told this joke many times before, but it was funny anyway. He always got excited about his speakers.

We settled into a quiet reverie, me fondly remembering the party at its wildest, Doug perhaps imagining what it would have been like had he bothered to attend.

"I heard you went out to a club the other night," I said.

"Yeah."

"Good for you!" I said. "Who'd you see?"

"Oh, I don't remember. Some band I read about in the *Stranger*. I stood next to this guy in a wheelchair. It was kind of amazing that he was there. He couldn't see the stage. I talked to him for a little bit. He seemed pretty cool. Then I came home. I don't like to go out to drink. I never drive drunk."

"You didn't hit on any women?" I asked. Ever since he had broken up with his boyfriend, Doug had never talked about men, only women. I tried to play along.

"No," he said.

"I don't really get out to many shows these days," I said, "but I still have my favorite bars. There's the Jade Pagoda and—hey, you should try going to the Twilight Exit. That's within walking distance." I pointed south.

"Isn't that where all the—" He trailed off, as if I were supposed to know what he meant. I did. There was a street corner on Madison where a lot of poor black people loitered and police cruised by. A drug corner, one of a handful in the city.

"No," I said. "That's a block or so to the east, by that little grocery store."

"But why would you go by there?"

I considered my response, skipping political correctness to appeal to Doug's pragmatism. "Well, you know, you really aren't in much danger. For one, the cops are there all the time. For another, white people don't get mugged on street corners like that. If people got robbed there, people would stop coming to buy drugs."

"I guess so," Doug said. We both looked out towards the street. Then Doug said, "I once broke a guy's nose."

"What? Why?"

"He kicked my cat."

The air shifted. We were both uncomfortable.

Doug had finished his cigarette. He rocked back and forth on his heels, his heavy body swaying to an unknown rhythm. I studied the cracks on the porch railing. The house needed a paint job. It was like we were sitting in the shade of a two-story lump of green-gray earth, a blotted vein of exposed moss and minerals.

"So how's work?" Doug asked.

"Work?" I said. "You mean, you don't know?"

Doug gave a shrug.

"I got fired."

"Really? *A-a-a-a-a-a-hh, du-u-u-u-u-u-de,*" he said. "Jesus! I'm sorry." His words came out like dirty oil dripping out of an automobile. Doug usually ended his sentences on a downbeat, as if nothing could interest him. This time, his stressors slid in the other direction. Doug worked for a roofing contractor, and he didn't identify very strongly

with the job. But he knew how important my reporting career had
been to me.

He looked away. We both did. "Do you want a beer?" he asked.

"Sure, man. Thanks."

"Come on."

We went upstairs. Doug motioned for me to be careful because
he didn't want to disturb the piranhas. If you opened the door to his
room too fast, they'd lunge around in their tank as if their very lives
were at stake. It would take close to a minute for the water to return
to a placid, aquarium state. I trailed Doug inside with a tiptoed,
exaggerated caution.

"What'd you feed them this week?" I said, pointing with the
bottle of beer he'd given me. I could see the piranhas' lower rows of
teeth, jagged saws that could tear through other fish, hamburger meat,
even human flesh. Whenever those saws were so clearly visible, I had
learned, they had just eaten.

"I think last night they ate one of the other fish. See? Only three
of the other ones left."

"Huh. I wasn't counting."

"After you've seen them do it half a dozen times, it gets boring."
We stared at the fish together. They were more mesmerizing than the
traffic. Doug looked at me, suddenly feverish. "Hey, did I tell you
what I'm gonna do next?"

"No." I breathed, still. "What?"

"I'm going to breed the piranhas."

"*Breed* them."

"Aw, yeah, dude! I mean, you know these things are illegal, right?"

I did. He had already bragged about how he had persuaded a
pet store owner in an unnamed part of town to show him the store's
"secret back room" where the "real" pets were kept.

"So this guy and I are friends now, right? He told me if I bred this
pair of piranhas, I could sell them for at *least* fifty dollars a fish. All I
gotta do is raise a whole bunch of them. I could make thousands!" At
this Doug let out a crazy-cooter guffaw. He didn't slap his knee with
his giant hand, though I had actually seen him do that before.

"I'm going to need a bigger tank, of course, and that's going to be the hardest part. Fish tanks are expensive. I might have to take a job on the weekends to pay for it."

"Doug, how big of a tank are we talking about?" I passed my empty bottle back to him. He went back to the refrigerator and got me another. I normally wouldn't have done this—expected another beer—because Doug's gifts of alcohol struck me as a form of reluctant charity, not altruism. But today we were getting along.

"I want a hundred-gallon tank."

"One *hundred* gallons? Jesus. How big is that?"

With his arms, Doug showed me. It was a wider span than his limbs could display.

"Are you sure the landlady's okay with this?" I said. His room was a mess, with an odd assortment of DVDs, gadgets, tools, and bicycle parts covering every available square foot of floor and shelf. Where would he put a giant fish tank? I tried to imagine what would happen to the room if the earthquake they called the 'Big One' hit Seattle.

"Listen, don't worry about that!" he snapped, suddenly touchy. "I've *talked* to her."

"All right. OK." We both knew this was a lie, but I let it pass. Since he had taken the trouble to lie to me, he was going to have to accept the blame if the landlady ever found out.

"Let's go downstairs. I need another smoke." He looked like he didn't want me in his room anymore. We returned to the porch.

I leaned on the railing overlooking the street. Doug went into his patient find-and-light-a-cigarette routine. When he had situated himself, he handed me a piece of paper from his pocket.

"What's this?" I said.

"I found it stuck in the mail slot."

It was a brochure, the amateurish kind I normally threw out without reading. Somebody was promoting a lawn mowing service. "*This* was on the porch?" I asked.

"Yeah."

"Fucking, passive-aggressive, fucking-ass neighbors," I said. "I hate this town. I mowed the goddamn lawn."

"Last month," Doug said.

"Hey," I said. "This isn't entirely my problem. Anybody can mow the lawn. It's not my job to mow the lawn. Even SnowWolf can mow the lawn—why don't you get on his case sometime? He never does any chores. It took me three months to persuade the landlady to let me buy a new lawn mower because none of us wanted to use that crappy manual push mower that we used to have. So I got us a new mower, and it works, and anybody can mow the lawn now, not just me."

Doug was itching for an argument, I could tell, but despite his size he was even worse with conflict than I was. I held my ground, staring right at him so he knew I wasn't afraid of him.

"I'll do it if you want," he muttered. "It's no big deal."

"No," I said. "I don't want you to do it just because I want you to do it. I want people to pitch in and do things of their own free will around here."

"Nobody's going to do it then."

"Then I'll put up a sign-in sheet in the kitchen. People sign up for a particular time when they'll mow the lawn. We'll get it done. And fuck the neighbors. That sounds pretty fair to me, don't you think?"

Doug gave up with a shrug.

I turned to go back inside. As I opened the front door, I thanked Doug for the beer.

"Sure," he said. "Any time." Behind me I could hear my housemate throwing his empty into the glass-recycling bin. He hurled it so hard the glass shattered.

ANN COLE BROWN

WHEN LESS IS MORE: THE AUTHOR'S VOICE IN NON-FICTION WRITING

Ann Cole Brown
When Less is More: The Author's Voice in Non-Fiction Writing

WORKSHOP DESCRIPTION

Often under-appreciated, the author's voice plays a central role in successful non-fiction writing. Careful and conscious crafting of the writer's voice can turn an average piece of non-fiction into a memorable work. Learn how to identify and control the critical elements that establish the author's voice and create successful non-fiction.

INSTRUCTOR BIOGRAPHY

Ann Cole Brown teaches writing at the University of Pennsylvania. For thirty years she has taught students of all ages to find their ideas and voices through writing. She is also a writer and editor and the co-author of two series of textbooks, *Houghton Mifflin Grammar* and *Houghton Mifflin English*.

JOSEPH CONLIN

SUBMITTING TO THE LITERARY MAGAZINE

Joseph Conlin
Submitting to the Literary Magazine

WORKSHOP DESCRIPTION

Submitting and getting published in any of the variety of literary journals builds what the agents and publishers are calling a platform. The platform makes it easier for agents and editors to wade through the reams of material they receive daily from writers around the world. It also makes it easier for them and the writer to promote any new work. Why should you get your short stories, poems, or essays published in these small and sometimes obscure journals? How do you get published in these journals? How should you submit? What should you submit? What are submission guidelines and do they matter? Will someone steal my work, my idea? What are editors looking for? What does an editor face when reading the material? Why don't editors/readers comment on your work? What did the editor by this and that in a rejection letter? Where are there sources for literary publications? What motivates the editor of a literary journal? In other words, why do hundreds of individuals work for nothing or close to nothing to publish fiction, poetry, and essays in publications that maybe a 1000 people read? What are the advantage/disadvantages of publishing in an online publication versus a traditional publication?

INSTRUCTOR BIOGRAPHY

Joseph Conlin has spent three decades in the publishing/writing field, but it wasn't until the 1990s that he dove full-time into the literary marketplace. His short stories have appeared in such publications as *Maryland Review, Fairfield Review, Algonquin Roundtable Review, small spiral notebook, Sulphur River Review,* and *Hob-Nob Review.* His essays have appeared in a variety of business magazines. A publisher is considering his novel, *Orlando Tales.* Since 1999, he has edited and published the literary magazine *SNReview* (www.snreview.org). Conlin also teaches English and creative writing at the University of Bridgeport and Sacred Heart University and is a mentor in Western Connecticut State University's MFA writing program. He has an MFA in Creative Writing from Goddard College.

CHARIS CONN

AN EDITOR'S GUIDE TO EDITING AND SUBMISSIONS

Charis Conn
An Editor's Guide to Editing and Submissions

WORKSHOP DESCRIPTION

Editing can be the difference between a good story and great one, and it can be almost as impossible for us to do alone as it is to find others to do it effectively. This workshop will focus on the strategies of self-editing and of seeking, assessing, and using editing by others. We will examine the most common fatal flaws made by beginning fiction writers, and consider some ways to find and eliminate them. Commonly missed opportunities in fiction will also be reviewed. The value and availability of every kind of editing will be discussed, as well as how fiction manuscripts are handled by national magazines and their editors.

INSTRUCTOR BIOGRAPHY

Charis Conn's short stories have appeared in *the North American Review, New Letters,* and in *Harper's Magazine* where she edited and wrote fiction, articles, and the *Harper's Index* for twenty years. Her first novel, *Through the Green Fuse,* will be published by Pantheon in 2008. She has taught fiction writing at the Santa Barbara, Cape Cod, and Bread Loaf writers' conferences, as well as at the universities of California, Southern Maine, and Pennsylvania. She currently teaches at New York's Gotham Writers' Workshop and at Syracuse University. She is also a Contributing Editor of *Harper's Magazine.*

LIZ CORCORAN

CHARACTER—THE BEGINNING FICTION WRITER'S BUILDING BLOCK

Liz Corcoran
Character—The Beginning Fiction Writer's Building Block

WORKSHOP DESCRIPTION

Just starting out as a fiction writer and looking for a way to begin creating stories? Start by creating a character and often you'll find the story soon follows. This beginning workshop will focus on the essential building blocks of fiction—characters—and how to begin creating well-rounded, interesting ones. We will discuss the importance of character within fiction writing and through a series of in-class exercises; students will work on creating characters of their own, and then identify the interesting elements in the character's "life" which can be used to develop a story.

INSTRUCTOR BIOGRAPHY

Liz Corcoran is the Director of the MFA in Creative Writing program of the School of Graduate and Continuing Studies at Rosemont College. She received her M.A. in Creative Writing from Temple University. Her most recent short story, "An Hour at the Station," appeared in Oasis. She is currently working on a novel about stand-up comedians and a collection of stories that examines modern interpretations of magic. Liz also teaches literature and writing at Temple and Drexel Universities and serves as the Managing Director for Rev Theatre Company.

NANNETTE CROCE

BREAKING INTO EZINES

SUPPLEMENTARY MATERIALS:

HANDOUT: THE TOP TEN REASONS *NOT* TO SUBMIT
TO EZINES

Nannette Croce
Breaking Into Ezines

WORKSHOP DESCRIPTION

Online literary magazines (ezines) reach an international audience and the best ones can attract hundreds of thousands of hits per issue. Once considered a second choice to print, ezines are becoming more and more popular as writers see the advantages of a wider audience and having their work archived online. In this workshop we will explore the differences between writing for ezines and print and talk about ways writers can leverage those differences to their benefit. We'll review some recently published ezine pieces to determine what caught the editor's eye. Finally, we'll discuss how writers can find the best ezine markets for their work and formatting and etiquette for online submissions. Those who register for the class may submit one short story or essay of no more than 2500 words up to one week prior to the workshop for critique and consideration for publication in The Rose & Thorn Literary Ezine *www.theroseandthornezine. com.* The instructor will contact registrants regarding how to submit their manuscripts. Work from non-registrants will not be accepted. Beginner/intermediate level.

INSTRUCTOR BIOGRAPHY

Nannette Croce is Senior Prose Editor for *The Rose & Thorn Literary Ezine www.theroseandthornezine.com* Established in 1998, this award-winning ezine receives over 300,000 hits per month and publishes fiction, essays, and poetry from all over the world. The Rose &Thorn has been named one of the "101 Best Websites for Writers" and an "Internet Envy Site" by *Writer's Digest.* In addition to her work at *The Rose & Thorn*, Nannette writes a weekly column on Aboriginal

History for *Suite 101.com* and her fiction and nonfiction have appeared in various print and online publications including *The Philadelphia Inquirer, Montana, the Magazine of Western History,* and, of course, *The Rose and Thorn.*

The Top Ten Reasons *Not* to Submit to Ezines

1. You like buying pretty stamps.
2. You have a crush on the guy/gal at the post office.
3. You like waking in the middle of the night wondering if you included an SASE with your last submission—hey, it's a good time to get some work done on that next submission.
4. You hate trees.
5. You worry about the Postal Service going under (see # 2) and have no problem sending out SASEs you'll never see again.
6. You like knowing that you and your dear mama are most likely the only ones who will ever read your published story again.
7. You find it exciting not knowing exactly whose desk—if any—your submission will land on.
8. You prefer mailing photocopied clips to sending a URL in an email (see #1 and #5).
9. You prefer that only a handful of people living in the United States read your work.
10. You think that finding page 10 stuck in the printer after you've already posted your submission is hilariously funny and will make a great story over the water cooler.

If you answered yes to at least five of the above, perhaps ezines are not for you.

If you answered yes to three or less, why not give it a try?

If you don't know what an ezine is, fuggetaboutit.

ANN DE FOREST

READING AS A WRITER

Ann de Forest
Reading as a Writer

WORKSHOP DESCRIPTION

All writers began as readers. The books we loved introduced us to the power of language and enticed us to explore the possibilities of creating worlds with words. Sometimes, though, we writers regard reading as a distraction from the task at hand. Even worse, reading, once our greatest pleasure, can engender feelings of envy and competition. This workshop presents reading as a stimulating, ongoing apprenticeship for writers, providing endless opportunities to hone our craft by turning to the masters who inhabit our bookshelves and local libraries. We will discuss practical matters such as how to incorporate reading into your writing schedule and how to set up a reader's notebook, and we will explore the value of "imitation" and "annotation" and other methods of active, engaged reading that will make novice and expert alike better writers. Through in-class exercises, participants will solve craft problems particular to their own writing, using authors that they regard as models, influences, or inspiration. Please bring to class a work-in-progress, two different samples from authors you admire, and a blank notebook.

INSTRUCTOR BIOGRAPHY

Ann de Forest's fiction has appeared in *Timber Creek Review*, *Open City*, and *Pif*, and been performed at Writing Aloud, Philadelphia's theatrical showcase for short stories. As a journalist and design critic, she has contributed feature stories, essays and reviews to a range of newspapers and magazines, including the *New York Times*, the *Philadelphia Inquirer*, *Navigator*, *ID: The Magazine of International Design*, and *Attachè, US Airways*. Opportunity grants from the Pennsylvania Council for the Arts and a fellowship at Vermont Studio

Center supported work on *The World Writers*, her forthcoming trilogy for middle-grade readers. A former lecturer at the Cooper-Hewitt Museum, she is currently resident writer and liberal arts critic for the senior graphic design studio at University of the Arts.

BARBARA DECESARE

**WHAT WE TALK ABOUT WHEN WE TALK
ABOUT LOVE**
*WHAT WE TALK ABOUT WHEN WE TALK
ABOUT LOVE*

Barbara DeCesare
What We Talk About When We Talk About Love
What We Talk About When We Talk About Love

WORKSHOP DESCRIPTION

In this workshop, we'll delve into the secrets of character and dialog that work magic throughout Carver's collection of short stories *What We Talk About When We Talk About Love*. We'll examine the literary condition that made Carver's voice so distinct and so welcome, and we'll also undertake exercises in recovering important characters from our own lives; ones we haven't thought about in many years.

INSTRUCTOR BIOGRAPHY

Short fiction by **Barbara DeCesare** has won some cash (Grain, others) and been adopted for film (Columbia Film School, Chicago). Barbara is a former book review editor (Wordhouse, Baltimore) whose poetry was adapted for stage last year at the Midtown International Theatre Festival in NYC (Dreamhouse). She continues work on her first screenplay (Low Grade Fever) and CD (Up to my Ass in Diamonds) while seeking help for her debilitating parenthesis habit.

TOM DEVANEY

IN THE REALM OF THE SENSES:
ASPECTS OF DESCRIPTIVE WRITING

Tom Devaney
In the Realm of the Senses: Aspects of Descriptive Writing

WORKSHOP DESCRIPTION

This workshop is intended for writers of any genre: fiction, poetry, nonfiction who wishes to sharpen their descriptive writing skills. Conveying a place, a work of art, a character, an experience or an event through your writing involves paying close attention to the details by using all of your five senses. We will focus on a two-fold approach towards describing and description: 1) seeing and making keen observations and 2) creating an evocative experience on the page for your readers. This interactive workshop includes handouts and writing techniques to hone your descriptive skills. Please bring in fourteen (14) copies of one page of a favorite descriptive passage from any author. Please include the name of the piece and author on each page as well as your own name. Also, please bring in fourteen (14) copies of one to two pages of your own work (an essay, story, or short poem) to discuss the possibilities of descriptive writing.

INSTRUCTOR BIOGRAPHY

Thomas Devaney is poet, essayist, and Penn Senior Writing Fellow in English Department for the Critical Writing Program at the University of Pennsylvania. He is the author of *The American Pragmatist Fell in Love* (Banshee Press, 1999) and *Letters to Ernesto Neto* (Germ Folios, 2005). In the summer of 2004 he conducted a series of tours of the Edgar Allan Poe National Historic Site called "The Empty House" for The Institute of Contemporary Art's show "The Big Nothing." Devaney's poems have been published in *The American Poetry Review*, *Fence*, *Jacket*, and in the anthologies *Walt Whitman, Hom(m)age, 2005/1855* (Turtle Point Press, 2005) and *American Poetry: The Next Generation* (Carnegie Mellon, 2000). His poems and essays have also been translated into French and published in *Arsenal, Java, Poesie,* and *Double Change.* His articles and essays have been published in *The Philadelphia Inquirer, Poets & Writers, The Boston Review,* and *Rain Taxi.*

SUZÉ DIPIETRO

LIGHTS! CAMERA! ACTION!
LET THE PUBLICITY BEGIN!

Suzé DiPietro
Lights! Camera! Action! Let The Publicity Begin!

WORKSHOP DESCRIPTION

So you have just gotten your book published . . . Now the fun begins! Whether or not you have a professional publicist or are going to be doing the job yourself, there are certain things you must know in order to get the word out about you and your book! This course will teach you how to 'pitch' yourself and your book. In class, you will learn how to put together a press release and publications to contact. You will develop your story 'angle' and learn how journalists like to be contacted.

INSTRUCTOR BIOGRAPHY

Suzé DiPietro is a highly regarded publicity maven, writer and speaker. During her tenure as Corporate Director of Public Relations at the Trump Hotels and Casino Resorts, she worked with the some of the world's biggest film and rock stars, including George Clooney, Sarah Jessica Parker, Leonardo DiCaprio, Sting, Beyonce and Stone Temple Pilots. She negotiated on-site filming at Trump properties, including *Sex and the City, Ocean's 11* and Woody Allen's *Celebrity*. She also developed and coordinated all PR plans, budgets and media for Trump Resort executives, including Donald Trump. She founded the VH1 Save the Music Auction at the Trump Marina in 1999. In May 2005, Ms. DiPietro produced and headed up publicity for the "Oh . . . So Wilde" Fashion Show hosted by Johnny Rzeznik of the Goo Goo Dolls to raise money for VH1 Save the Music Foundation. Ms. DiPietro has an extensive background in the theatre as well, working as the Marketing and Public Relations Director at the Merriam Theater in Philadelphia and now the Stockton Performing Arts Center in New Jersey. At the Merriam Theater, she was responsible for creating and administering the marketing budgets and coordinating the PR for all the major Broadway tours, including *The Producers, Oklahoma!* and *Movin' Out.* She has worked extensively with the national media, including *The New York Times, Philadelphia Inquirer, 48 Hours, CBS Nightly News, MTV, VH1, The Oprah Winfrey Show* and *The View.* Ms. DiPietro is the author of An Angel Knocks on Hell's Door and will release her second book in the fall. She is a University of Pennsylvania graduate.

TYLER DOHERTY

HYBRID FORMS: THE HAIBUN

Tyler Doherty
Hybrid Forms: The Haibun

WORKSHOP DESCRIPTION

Pioneered by the great wanderer-poet Matsuo Bashō on his 156-day trek through the wilds of 17th century Japan, the haibun remains a vibrant form to this day. Equally adaptable to such diverse genres as memoir, nature writing, travel journal, and daybook, the haibun combines condensed, elliptical prose with the startling, imagistic juxtapositions of haiku. In this workshop, we will read from a wide variety of haiku and haibun practitioners—from ancients like Bashō, Buson and Issa, to New American and Post-Avant moderns like Joanne Kyger, Gary Snyder, Andrew Schelling and Hoa Nguyen. Mining our experience for minute particulars and luminous details, we will also write some haibun of our own and learn to apply strategies for revising our work. This workshop is ideally suited for prose writers interested in short shorts and hybrid forms, as well as poets looking to branch out into prose.

INSTRUCTOR BIOGRAPHY

Tyler Doherty was born in Toronto, Canada and lives in the Germantown section of Philadelphia. He holds an MFA in Writing and Poetics from Naropa University and an M. ED from Arcadia University. His first book, *Bodhidharma Never Came to Hatboro*, was published by Bootstrap Press in 2004. Recent poems have appeared magazines including *Shiny, Hot Whiskey, the@ttacheddocument*, and *Streetnotes*. His work was also anthologized in the *Wisdom Anthology of North American Buddhist Writing* edited by Andrew Schelling. Co-founder of the Young Writers Project, which conducts innovative writing workshops with Philadelphia youth, he teaches in the English Department at Arcadia University where he is also the Director of the Writing Center.

GREG DOWNS

WRITING HISTORICAL FICTION

Greg Downs
Writing Historical Fiction

WORKSHOP DESCRIPTION

Although many writers think of historical fiction as a genre, many great literary novels are not only set in the past but deal fundamentally with the meaning of the past in the present. Of the five books that received the most votes in *The New York Times'* best book of the last 25 years poll, all five were explorations of the past, as are many prize-winning novels from the last few years, including *Gilead, The Known World,* and *March.* Rather than a sideline for genre specialists, writing fiction about history has been a central concern for our best writers, like Morrison, Roth, Updike, and Edward Jones. In this class, we will use examples drawn from those writers and Michael Ondaatje's historical fiction, to discuss the art and craft of historical fiction. Particularly, we will discuss the complexities of balancing research and fiction, and the complex process of letting the images and meaning of the story take precedence over abstract ideas about the past. Bring a idea for a novel or a beginning of your novel, the name of your favorite historical novel, and a notebook for some quick in-class writing.

INSTRUCTOR BIOGRAPHY

Greg Downs' book of short stories, *Spit Baths,* won the Flannery O'Connor Award and was published in October 2006 by the University of Georgia Press. His stories have appeared in many literary magazines, including *Glimmer Train, New Letters, Black Warrior Review, Meridian, Southeast Review, Sycamore Review, CutBank,* and *Philadelphia Stories.* An historical novel, which he is currently revising, won the Iowa Writers' Workshop's James Michener Award. Along with an MFA from the Iowa Writers' Workshop, Greg has a Ph.D. in History from the University of Pennsylvania, and is an Assistant Professor of History at the City College of New York.

TONYA M. EVANS-WALLS

PROTECTING YOUR COPYRIGHT IN THE DIGITAL AGE

Tonya M. Evans-Walls
Protecting Your Copyright in the Digital Age

WORKSHOP DESCRIPTION

Everyone knows that if it's posted on the Internet then it must be in the public domain and free, right? WRONG! However, new technologies and the Internet have certainly stretched existing copyright law to its limit. This exciting and engaging course will explore the benefits and challenges of creating and protecting your literary work in this digital age and answer your most pressing questions about how to benefit from unprecedented access by to the public to your work and also how to prevent (or at least reducing) the likelihood of infringement. How does copyright law protect your online content—sample chapters, poetry, articles, websites and newsletters? What kind of legal trouble could you unknowingly invite with your blog or message board? This workshop presents need-to-know information that every writer who is serious about his or her writing career should be aware of in the digital age.

INSTRUCTOR BIOGRAPHY

Attorney **Tonya M. Evans-Walls**, Esq., practices in the areas of entertainment law, intellectual property, estate planning, and municipal finance. Co-chair of the Pennsylvania Bar Association Sports, Entertainment and Art Law committee, she is a nationally recognized speaker on publishing and intellectual property law and estate planning issues. A poet and writer, she is the author of numerous books, including *Literary Law Guide for Authors: Copyright, Trademark, and Contracts in Plain Language, Seasons of Her* and *SHINE!* Her short story, "Not Tonight," appears in the anthology *Proverbs for the People* (Kensington). Prior to law school, Mrs. Evans-Walls competed on the women's professional tennis circuit and played in the US Open,

Virginia Slims of Philadelphia, and Lipton in 1993. She lives in Philadelphia with her husband, O. Russel Walls, III, and is a member of Alpha Kappa Alpha Sorority, Inc.

JANET RUTH FALON

JOURNALING FOR WRITERS

Janet Ruth Falon
Journaling for Writers

WORKSHOP DESCRIPTION

A journal/diary is the perfect place to support and nourish your more public writing, to mull over issues of content and style and deal with the vicissitudes of the writing process. In this workshop, you will learn and practice techniques that will help you break through to a new level of dynamic journaling while you simultaneously grapple with essential questions about the writing life.

INSTRUCTOR BIOGRAPHY

Janet Ruth Falon, the author of *The Jewish Journaling Book* (Jewish Lights, 2004) is an award-winning poet, journalist, essayist, and writing teacher who has kept a journal for more than 40 years. Her work has appeared in numerous publications including *The New York Times, The Philadelphia Inquirer,* and *The Boston Globe.* One of her essays was published in the anthology, *Father: Famous Writers Celebrate the Bond Between Father and Child* (Pocket Books).

GARY FINCKE

THE FIRST-PERSON NARRATOR:
THE IMPORTANCE OF VOICE

SUPPLEMENTARY MATERIALS:

EXCERPT: *ALL SQUARE*

Gary Fincke
The First-Person Narrator: The Importance of Voice

WORKSHOP DESCRIPTION

The course will emphasize how a distinct, first-person narrator who is genuinely "heard" can make a short story memorable. A variety of opening pages of first-person narrative will be employed, and students will be asked to produce an opening page of first-person narration to discuss. The heart of this course will be that how the story is told is as important as the story itself.

INSTRUCTOR BIOGRAPHY

Gary Fincke is the Writers Institute Director as well as Professor of English and Creative Writing at Susquehanna University. Winner of the 2003 Flannery O'Connor Award for Short Fiction and the 2003 Ohio State University/The Journal Poetry Prize for recent collections of stories and poems, he has published nineteen books of poetry, short fiction, and nonfiction, most recently *Standing Around the Heart* (poems, Arkansas, 2005), *Sorry I Worried You* (stories, Georgia, 2004), and *Amp'd: A Father's Backstage Pass*, a nonfiction account of his son's life as a rock guitarist in the band Breaking Benjamin (Michigan State, 2004). *Standing around the Heart* was a finalist for the 2006 Paterson Poetry Prize.

Winner of the Bess Hokin Prize from *Poetry* Magazine and the Rose Lefcowitz Prize from *Poet Lore*, Dr. Fincke has received a PEN Syndicated Fiction Prize as well as seven fellowships for creative writing from the Pennsylvania Council on the Arts. His poems, stories, and essays have appeared in such periodicals as *Harper's, Newsday, The Paris Review, The Kenyon Review, The Georgia Review, American Scholar,* and *Doubletake*. Twice awarded Pushcart Prizes for his work and cited nine times in the past ten years for a "Notable Essay" in *Best American Essays*, Dr. Fincke's essay "The Canals of Mars" was reprinted in *The Pushcart Essays*, an anthology of the best nonfiction printed during the first twenty-five years of the Pushcart Prize volumes.

An excerpt from Gary Fincke's short story
ALL SQUARE

During my junior year in high school, a month after my mother moved in with a man named Jim Allison, my father, who taught social studies to seniors, was fired. He'd beaten a student. Had found him out and taken him into a faculty bathroom and punched him a dozen times. "I want a word with you" was what my father had said to the boy, and he'd locked the door behind him. He didn't know the boy. Later, he would say if he'd known him he wouldn't have beaten him. "He was a stranger," my father explained. "Knowing a boy would keep me from that."

The boy had punched another teacher. A woman. He'd said, "I hope you have a baby in there," laying his fist into her stomach.

"Unacceptable," my father said. "Absolutely." He'd been working at that school for twenty-four years and had never touched another student, but the superintendent said he had no choice. The boy's family agreed not to press charges if my father was fired. The boy, whose name was Jessie Grant, was suspended for ten days, the longest the school could keep someone away without providing home tutoring, and he agreed to go to anger management sessions. The woman wasn't pregnant, but she called in sick the following day and didn't come back for any one of those ten days the boy was gone.

The teacher's union filed a grievance, but my father didn't protest. "When you see the terribly wrong," he told me, "it's not about choosing. You act or you're with the other team."

My father had played semi-pro football until I was born and was fond of sports analogies. I took this one to mean he thought the other team had a full lineup, and I couldn't disagree. "I don't count myself special," he went on, but I had to attend that school every day for another year and two months.

For two days no one said anything about my father to me at school. It was like the year before when Joel Eberly had chemotherapy, and he walked around for a week by himself. When a teacher finally called on him, I was surprised Joel's voice sounded the same as it had before his treatments.

On the third day, before home room, two women teachers I'd never had for class paused beside my locker as I pulled out my morning books. "We want you to know we appreciate your father," the younger one said.

I knew her name was Miss Scott and that she taught Spanish. "Ok," I said.

The other one, whose name I didn't know, glanced into my locker as if she expected to get to know me better by looking at my books. "You're a junior here, aren't you?" she said.

"Yes," I said, and I closed the door.

"You keep your head up," Miss Scott said. I shifted the books to my right hand and waited. "There's no shame," she added, and both of them turned away.

When I opened my locker before lunch, there was a note stuck in the door. "Your father is a piece of shit," it said, and I wondered, balling it up in my hand, whether it had been written by a student or a teacher. When I walked into the cafeteria, Mike Fernald waved me over to my regular table. "What's up?" he said, as if I'd been absent for two days.

The next Sunday my mother called. "I wasn't sure you'd be home," she said. "I thought your father might be making you a churchgoer now, but I at least was sure he'd be in that pew of his."

"Third row, aisle seat," I said. "I went with him last Sunday because of all the trouble."

"I'm sorry for you," she said. "You keep that to yourself, though."

"Ok."

"We're both of us fools," she said. "Ed might think he's walking a different path, but they both end up at the same place."

"He doesn't talk about you, Mom. Honest."

"Yes, he does, Jeff. He comes through your front door talking."

"He hardly talks at all." It sounded like a confession, like I wished for her and her drinking to be back in the house because it needed another voice.

"You'll learn, Jeff. After a while, you won't be able to hear yourself think for all the talking he does with his body."

I looked at the clock that sat on top of the closet where the good dishes and silverware were displayed as if they were for sale. I'd given my mother that clock for Christmas the year before, and right then it said 11:18, so I knew my father was listening to a sermon while I waited for my mother to finish.

My father took a job at the anchor store at the mall. He sold gardening equipment and supplies—lawnmowers, hedge clippers, weed-whackers. Selling those was easy, my father explained. Customers either bought the good stock or they scraped by with the low-end.

It was fertilizers and weed killers and bags of mysterious nutrients that were problems. People wanted to know what to expect from using these things, and all my father could say was what was already written on the box or bag. The store sold six kinds of grass seed, for instance—did one kind really do better in full sun? And all those ground covers and perennials to be expert about—partial sun, full sun, full shade; acidic soil, alkaline soil. He'd never done anything but cut grass every Saturday morning from April to October and trim the hedges three times a summer, an all-day job with his hand-held shears. He'd never even held electric garden tools. "It's not much different than teaching," he said. "You talk with assurance, and people will believe you."

The larger problem for him was people he knew coming into the store. Or worse, students with their parents, teenagers being dragged away from the CD or DVD racks to where their fathers were helping to pick out plants for overdue Easter presents or early Mother's Day gifts. "Those boys look like they're holding cigarettes behind their backs when they see me," he said. "They act like I've just opened the boys' room door."

My father and I began feeling our way into household tasks. It was easier than I imagined to believe we were doing well at keeping house, mostly because my mother had done such a lousy job. I knew to separate whites from all the dark colors for laundry because I'd been carrying the baskets for years. I knew where the dishwasher detergent was and how to iron shirts because they were already my jobs.

My father had taken to cleaning and dusting and making sure, as he put it, everything was ship-shape. I thought he was pleased with his work, that he understood the house looked better now that my mother was gone. He ran the vacuum every other day. "We should paint the living room," he said three weeks after he'd been fired, and he pointed out small scuff marks near the baseboards, a few smudges by the light switches, and a series of dark smears where chairs had been scraped along one wall.

He said that after a month he could get an employee discount at the department store where he worked. He had hours of extra time each night. He didn't have any tests to correct, and it seemed like I was becoming a boy who didn't need much talking to. "Your mother was always upset about something," he said. "It slowed things down. Here we are getting right after everything."

I'd just finished ironing two weeks worth of dress shirts for him, and he examined the shirts on their hangers, the collars and the sleeves, and then the fronts of each. I thought of him standing among two dozen lawnmowers in those shirts, his employee name tag clipped to a perfectly pressed pocket.

"Fine," he said. "these are fine."

He spread them apart in the closet as if wrinkles would set in them if they touched. "Christine never got the hang of ironing," he said. "She had a mind to send all my shirts and trousers out, but that didn't cut it."

"I'm ok with it, Dad," I said.

"Yes, we are," he said. "We're going to be fine."

A week later, a Saturday morning, he woke me early and told me to get in the car. I thought we were going for paint because the month was up, but he drove fifteen miles to the town where he'd grown up, the part where there were streets of houses that bordered the overpass for the thruway that looped around our town because somebody had figured a way to get a big chunk of it named as an historical district.

We'd driven past his old house fifty times, but I'd never been down the side streets that dead-ended into abandoned buildings where the highway had gone through. "I wanted you to see where I played football for Coach Kravick," he said, parking the car in a patch of knee-high grass. A few steps away, nearly under the overpass, the field my father played his home games on was still there—level and hard-packed and nearly entirely without grass. "Nobody cared much about making the grass grow," my father said. "I don't know if anybody still plays here, but it looks as if they do."

I stopped and got out, thinking my father would follow, but he stayed in the car. I walked toward the field, listening for the click of the car door latch, and when I didn't hear it, I made myself keep walking as if it was important for me to step onto that field.

The field, even in early May, was hard under my feet, the muddy patches shallow depressions in the unyielding surface. I looked up at the thruway, which appeared to be more weathered than I expected something like that to be when it was just eight years old. After I made it to the far sideline, I saw chunks of concrete, broken brick, and pieces of scrap metal lying in a patch of last year's thistle and milkweed. A gust of wind fluttered the sports section of a newspaper up against my ankles, and it looked so old I expected to see headlines about Bill Buckner's World Series error, something Coach Kravick would have used to motivate my father during his last season, telling him about playing through adversity. It was a mistake for my father to come here, I thought. It was like a high school reunion gone bad—classmates changing into older and uglier versions of who my father remembered. "Even with that road up there now, it's the same," my father said when I got back to the car. "It was always like playing at the ass-end of everything."

"It looks like a place a visiting team would hate to come to," I said.

My father smiled, and I thought I'd said something that would make a difference in the day. "If you'd played football, you'd know something about looking out for yourself," my father said then, and it sounded like I'd never spoken.

I kept my eyes on the field. "I'm ok, Dad," I said. I wanted my father to understand I wasn't afraid at school, but he was staring through the side window in a way that told me there weren't any words he wanted to hear.

"I'm talking about consequences," he said. "When they're all around you, there's something other than thinking that's called for."

He drove three blocks and parked again, but this time he left the motor running. Across the street was a bar called Tomko's.

"What's up?" I said. There were crime scene ribbons stretched across the front door.

"Coach Kravick got himself killed in there last night," my father said. "Drinking and money."

My father's last game had been seventeen years ago. I looked carefully at the small windows and the huge beer-advertisement banners. I wanted to get out and look around back, but unless my father opened his door, I couldn't move.

"Fats Kravick," he said. "He'd made a bet, and he had words with a man about not paying. Fats slapped the man, and that man went home, got a gun, came back, and killed him right there in Tomko's." My father stared at the door as if he expected to see Fats Kravick walk out with his arm over the shoulders of an old teammate. "A baseball bet," he said. "And here it is barely May."

I looked up at the thruway again, remembering that my father had told me traffic backed up for ten miles during rush hour because the main highway narrowed and ran through that town until I was eight years old. "Fats Kravick was a man you listened to," my father said, and then he added, "I think drinking must be something that closes your eyes in a fight."

I waited for him to go on, but I knew he meant me to remember my first boxing lesson, how I'd shut my eyes as his fists jabbed at me, and he stopped to tell me he already knew I wouldn't hit back. He flicked his fists near my face, telling me to keep my eyes open because anybody else would see his advantage with me and wade in to hurt me. "Your mother has her eyes closed," he said, and for a few seconds I fixed on that yellow ribbon. "You know," he said at last, "I've never allowed myself to take a drink because I was afraid I wouldn't be able to stop."

I'd had a few beers during my sophomore year, and lately I'd been drunk on most Saturday nights. I never thought about drinking on Monday or Tuesday. Drinking was like going to a football game. It was something to do for three or four hours because it was fun.

"When your mother calls," he asked me, "does she tell you about Jim Allison?"

"She doesn't call, Dad," I said, which was true in so far as I meant regularly. And she'd never mentioned Jim Allison.

"I wouldn't use my fists on your mother's new man. She asked for her mess. It's not my doing." My father nosed the car forward, swinging out in a way that nearly pointed us toward Tomko's. "I've seen this Jim Allison," he said, letting the car drift into the oncoming lane before he finally turned the wheel and brought us back. I thought he was going to say more, but he stopped, and I understood that he'd described Jim Allison in that one sentence, that he believed I knew everything I needed to know.

BOB FINEGAN

MAKING YOUR STORIES COMPELLING
FROM THE START

Bob Finegan
Making Your Stories Compelling from the Start

WORKSHOP DESCRIPTION

Whether you're writing a short story or a novel, you want to hook your readers from the start and keep them hungrily attentive to everything that is happening in your narrative. This workshop will examine various components of fiction that writers use to compel their readers from the very first sentence. Although special attention will be given to starting off strong by creating curiosity, tension or suspense, we will also be exploring ways to ensure that your stories have sufficient narrative drive, intellectual significance and emotional appeal for the long haul. We will look at how a few masters of the craft employ such elements as voice, point of view, character, dialogue and plot to create in the reader's mind what John Gardner called "a vivid and continuous dream."

INSTRUCTOR BIOGRAPHY

Robert Finegan grew up in West Chester, PA. He earned his B.A in English and History from the University of Delaware, and his M.F.A. in fiction writing from the University of Pittsburgh. His short stories have appeared in *The Greensboro Review, The Antietam Review, The Sun, River Styx,* and *The Other Side.* His story "Help Me with This" was nominated for a Pushcart Prize, and he received a 2001 Pennsylvania Council on the Arts Fellowship in Literature. He has taught fiction and creative non-fiction writing at The University of Pittsburgh, Drexel University and Rosemont College.

GREGORY FROST

TEN MISTAKES THAT WRITERS MAKE
(AND THEN SOME)

Gregory Frost
Ten Mistakes that Writers Make (and then some)

WORKSHOP DESCRIPTION

What's often taught in workshops covers basics that you need in order to begin, and maybe to complete a draft of your story. Rarely is the first draft the only one. More often, it's a roadmap for what you truly want to write. In this workshop I'll cover common mistakes that writers make and can easily fix, from the causes of writer's block in its myriad forms, to smart ways to revise your fiction for publication.

INSTRUCTOR BIOGRAPHY

Gregory Frost's latest book is *Attack Of The Jazz Giants & OtherStories*, published by Golden Gryphon Press. *Publisher's Weekly* said in a starred review, "Frost demonstrates his mastery of the short story form in what will surely rank as one of the best fantasy collections of the year." His most recent novel, *Fitcher's Brides* (Tor Books), was an International Horror Guild Award and World Fantasy Award Finalist. He has also been a finalist for the James Tiptree Award, Nebula Award, Theodore Sturgeon Memorial Award, and Hugo Award. His currently available stories include "The Prowl" in *Mojo:Conjure Stories*, edited by Nalo Hopkinson, "Tengu Mountain" in *The Faery Reel* edited by Terri Windling & Ellen Datlow, "Dub" in *Weird Trails*, edited by Darrell Schweitzer, and "So Coldly Sweet, So Deadly Fair" in *Weird Tales* magazine. See *http://www.goldengryphon.com/* for more information on *Attack Of The Jazz Giants*. For more about Gregory and his other work, visit *http://www.gregoryfrost.com*

LISE FUNDERBURG

TRANSCENDING THE NAVEL: HOW TO SQUEEZE UNIVERSAL MEANING OUT OF THE PERSONAL ESSAY

Lise Funderburg
Transcending the Navel:
How To Squeeze Universal Meaning out of the Personal Essay

WORKSHOP DESCRIPTION

All of us grapple with life's mysteries, wonders, and wackiness on a daily basis. But how do we successfully bring that experience to the page, how do we give it the texture and structure that will engage and resonate with readers? Through exercises and in-class readings, we'll explore components of the successful personal essay, possible topics, and the delicate balance between revelation and self-absorption. Participants should submit a writing sample of 1-3 pp. of nonfiction writing for class discussion.

INSTRUCTOR BIOGRAPHY

Lise Funderburg is a journalist, essayist, critic, creative writing instructor, and the author of *Black, White, Other: Biracial Americans Talk About Race and Identity* (William Morrow, 1994). She has written book reviews, essays, and feature articles for numerous publications, including *The Nation, The Philadelphia Inquirer, Quarterly Black Review, The New York Times, The Washington Post, Salon.com*, and *O: The Oprah Magazine*. Her honors include a Leeway Foundation grant, a 2003 Nonfiction Fellowship from the Pennsylvania Council on the Arts and a 2004 Puffin Foundation grant. She has been awarded residencies at The Blue Mountain Center and the MacDowell Colony. She is currently an instructor in creative nonfiction writing at the University of Pennsylvania. She has an M.A. in journalism from Columbia University and her work can be seen at *http://www. lisefunderburg.com*.

MOLLY GLICK

THE AUTHOR/AGENT RELATIONSHIP

Molly Glick
The Author/Agent Relationship

WORKSHOP DESCRIPTION

Literary agents have been described many ways: as gatekeepers, creative midwives, power brokers, and even "bad cops" to their author's "good cop" when it comes to dealing with editors. Why is an agent necessary, and how do you go about finding the right one for your project? This course will cover all aspects of the author/agent relationship, from figuring out which agents to approach, to writing a killer query letter—from deciding what kind of agent you want to work with, to deciphering the agreement they ask you to sign. The course will be broken down into four sections: whether to work with an agent, how to get an agent interested, what to expect from your collaboration with an agent, and a question and answer period.

INSTRUCTOR BIOGRAPHY

Mollie Glick is an agent at The Jean V. Naggar Literary Agency, Inc. After graduating from Brown University, she started her publishing career as a literary scout, advising foreign publishers regarding the acquisition of rights to American books. She then worked as an editor at the Crown imprint of Random House, before switching over to "the other side" in July, 2003. Mollie's list focuses on literary and commercial fiction, as well as non-fiction—she's a generalist, more interested in finding fresh, unique voices and smart, original perspectives than in sticking to a prescribed genre. She's very hands-on, working collaboratively with her authors to refine their manuscripts and proposals, then focusing on identifying just the right editors for the submissions.

SHARI GOLDHAGEN

PUTTING IT ON THE PAGE

SUPPLEMENTARY MATERIALS:

EXCERPT: *FAMILY AND OTHER ACCIDENTS*

Shari Goldhagen
Putting it on the Page

WORKSHOP DESCRIPTION

Lots of people think that they have a novel inside of them, but very few ever manage to get it out and into the world! Sometimes it's the seemingly insurmountable page count of long fiction that scares writers from typing those first words. Others abort projects a hundred pages in, when they find themselves miles off their original plot. Then there are the writers who jump from story to story, leaving dozens of broken pages in their wake once the initial excitement for an idea fades. In this course, we'll discuss techniques to help you get started, as well as those to keep you going. We'll talk about establishing good writing habits and schedules, exercises to re-invigorate your enthusiasm, as well as the things you CAN do on a project when you are absolutely too frustrated to type another word.

INSTRUCTOR BIOGRAPHY

Shari Goldhagen's first novel, *Family and Other Accidents*, was released from Doubleday in Spring 06. A native Ohioan, Shari holds a lot of writing degrees from Big Ten Schools in the Midwest: A journalism degree from Northwestern and an MFA from Ohio State. While writing Family, Shari stalked celebrities for The *National Enquirer*, *Life & Style* and *Celebrity Living Weekly*. She also received generous fellowships from Yaddo, MacDowell and the Ohioana Library Association. Shari currently lives in New York City where she teaches fiction and works as a freelance writer.

An Excerpt of Shari Goldhagen's
Family and Other Accidents, Doubleday 2006

They walk down JFK Street, passing the redbrick John F. Kennedy School of Government complex where Connor reports daily.

"I remember being a kid and getting totally freaked out by that Kennedy poster you used to have over your desk," Connor says, so sincere Jack feels the post-Mona-nostalgia phenomenon well in his throat. "That used to be your thing, right? You were going to be president?"

Jack stares at the brown-green water of the Charles and thinks about the Cuyahoga, his river.

"Something like that," he says, feeling old and stodgy in business-casual khakis and a button-down. Everyone looks about nineteen—girls with pierced navels peeking out of baby tees, guys with too-big jeans. It's not as though he's the oldest person tromping through the rain-softened ground, but he's definitely in the latter half. And he wonders where that line of youth resides and how he stumbled across to the other side, a place where the stars of sitcoms and romantic comedies are now a few years his junior instead of his senior.

"What happened?" Laine asks, and Jack can't tell if she's being polite or if she's genuinely interested.

"Sometime in law school, I guess I decided I wanted a Porsche instead." Jack smiles now because he does plan to yell at Connor later.

"Sounds reasonable." Laine's gray eyes flash something.

"I could still go for the whole Jack Kennedy image," Jack says.

"Would that make me Bobby?" Connor asks.

"Hey, I don't want to be Ethel," Laine says, swollen lips in a pout. "She looks like a horse. I want to be Jackie."

"Fine with me." Jack puts his arm around Laine and gives her a good-natured squeeze. In some parallel universe in his head, he lets his hand linger too long on her shoulder, maybe taps her ass when Connor isn't looking—shags her for the sport of it, because she goes by a stupid name, and she'll end up hurting his brother anyway. In this universe he lets her go. "You can be my Jackie anytime."

"All girls want to be Jackie," Laine says. "It's one of the things we're taught when we're growing up—be elegant, be loyal, wear really nice clothes."

Jack thinks Laine means girls other than her, not the smart, sexually aggressive ones getting their MBAs from Harvard. It's the girls like Mona who want to be Jackie, demure and pretty, good with children and the elderly. Or at least, that's what he thought Mona wanted.

"Naw, Lainey," Connor says. "You're not Jackie or Ethel, you're Carolyn Bessette and I'm John-John. We're the next generation of dead Kennedys."

"I like it." Laine reaches for Connor's hand and braids her long fingers with his long fingers. "I like it a lot. Doomed, but doomed in new and different ways."

Letting Connor and Laine walk ahead, Jack kicks stones at the clunky soles of their Dr. Martens.

"Still doomed," he mumbles.

For more information about *Family and Other Accidents* and Shari's current book tour, visit: sharigoldhagen.com

BETH GOLDNER

FINDING THE HYPOCRITE: BUILDING THREE-DIMENSIONAL FICTIONAL CHARACTERS

Beth Goldner
Finding The Hypocrite:
Building Three-Dimensional Fictional Characters

WORKSHOP DESCRIPTION

To write a novel or short story, your characters need to have layers and complexity. Because humans are by nature hypocrites, so should your characters be. Learn how to develop a character that is full of humanity (warts and all), ripe with complexity, far from stereotypical, and with a strong and unique voice. Learn how to make characters both likeable and/or unlikeable by exploring their hypocrisies. Learn how capitalizing on this human condition can richen your characters and make the reader sympathetic to them. Through in-class exercises and discussions, we'll learn how making a character a hypocrite is not a bad thing, and certainly not a black-and-white endeavor.

INSTRUCTOR BIOGRAPHY

Beth Goldner is the author of *The Number We End Up With* (Counterpoint Press, 2005) and *Wake: Stories* (Counterpoint Press, 2003). Her books have been well received by *The Boston Globe*, *The New York Times*, *Booklist*, *Library Journal*, *The Orlando Sentinel*, among others. Her short fiction has appeared in numerous publications, including *The Missouri Review*, *The Massachussetts Review*, *Literal Latte*, *StoryQuarterly*, and *The Blue Mesa Review*. For five years she has been selected for the Writing Aloud program, where actors bring contemporary fiction to life on stage, at the Interact Theatre in Philadelphia. She is a graduate of West Chester University. She is a managing editor for a medical journal in Center City, and is also Adjunct Faculty at Rosemont College in the MFA in Creative Writing program. She lives in Ardmore, and is at work on her second novel.

VIVIAN GREY

WRITE YOUR LIFE STORY

Vivian Grey
Write Your Life Story

WORKSHOP DESCRIPTION

Your personal experience is important. Transform your life experiences into a personal written legacy. In a relaxed, supportive atmosphere you will learn to organize topics, develop your creative ideas and turn them into a compelling story. This interactive workshop includes guides, handout and writing techniques to use to express yourself, as well as tips on how to make your story memorable. This four-hour workshop is for all ages—from Generation Xers to grandparents—as well as for aspiring and experienced writers of fiction and non-fiction.

INSTRUCTOR BIOGRAPHY

Vivian Grey is an author, educator, consulting editor and journalist. Little, Brown & Co., Penguin Putnam, and Grolier, among others, have published her award-winning biographies for young people. Her titles have been selected for numerous "Best Books" lists, including her book, *Moe Berg: The Spy Behind Home Plate*, which has been optioned for a film. An elected member of the New Jersey Literary Hall of Fame, she is the founder of Rutgers University's One-On-One Writer's Conference. She has an M.A. from Columbia University and teaches the workshops *Writing For The Children's Market; Jump Start Your Creative Writing;* and *Write Your Life Story*, at the University of Pennsylvania's College of General Studies.

DAVID GROFF

MASTERING THE PUBLISHING BUSINESS: AN INSIDER'S GUIDE FOR WRITERS

David Groff
Mastering the Publishing Business: An Insider's Guide for Writers

WORKSHOP DESCRIPTION

Taught by a New York editor and writer with 24 years experience in corporate publishing (Crown/Random House) and in independent consulting for publishers, agents, and private clients, this workshop offers writers an insider's roadmap to navigating the increasingly daunting publishing business. The workshop seeks to help you negotiate every element of book publishing, from mastering its editorial and marketing intricacies to developing salable projects, connecting with publishing's gatekeepers, and building an enduring career. In the workshop's second half, we'll discuss your query letters, book proposals, and sample chapters. Students will be required to submit materials via email two weeks before the workshop and will receive submission information upon enrollment in the workshop.

INSTRUCTOR BIOGRAPHY

David Groff is an editor, writer, and poet living in New York City. A graduate of Princeton and the Iowa Writers Workshop, he spent 12 years at Crown Publishers, where he published authors including Colin Harrison, Dave Barry, and Patrice Gaines, and for the last dozen years has been an independent editor and consultant working with authors published by Hyperion, Miramax, Morrow, Wiley and other houses. He also edits and consults for literary agents and private clients, and has published several books of his own, including a collection of poetry, *Theory of Devolution*.

GRETCHEN HAERTCH

BREAKING INTO MAGAZINES:
MARKET WHAT YOU KNOW

Gretchen Haertch
Breaking Into Magazines: Market What You Know

WORKSHOP DESCRIPTION

If you long to see your words in print in one of the more than 18,000 magazines published in the United States, this beginner's workshop is for you. Bring your ideas, along with a sharp pencil and paper, and let's get started. This hands-on workshop will show you how to analyze the editorial needs of magazines, define your personal focus, and refine your story ideas for multiple publications. You will use your own interests and knowledge to explore possible article ideas, from simple how-tos, to opinion pieces, to memoir-based narratives. If you want sound article ideas and a practical introduction to launching a freelance magazine writing career, this is it.

INSTRUCTOR BIOGRAPHY

Gretchen Haertsch has taught graduate and undergraduate writing classes at Arcadia University since 2006, including courses in Magazine Writing and Writing for Children. She gained her first magazine publishing credit while still an undergraduate at Pennsylvania State University when she wrote a profile on a student weightlifter and got it published in *Strength and Health* magazine the first time out. In the many years since, she has accumulated many publishing credits, including *People, Places, Plants Magazine, Garden Borders, MetroKids, Landmarks, Hopscotch, The Friend, Junior Trails, The Philadelphia Inquirer, The Daily Intelligencer*, and *The Bucks County Courier Times*. Gretchen has also written textbooks for Glencoe/McGraw-Hill. Before turning her interest to teaching the craft of writing, Gretchen had a career as a marketing and public relations professional. She received an M.A. in English from Arcadia University in 2002. She continues to write professionally for a diverse range of business clients and is currently working on a historical fiction novel for young adults.

THOMAS HEMMETER

MASKING AND UNMASKING THE TRUE SELF:
MANIPULATING DISTANCE IN MEMOIRS AND
PERSONAL SKETCHES

Thomas Hemmeter
Masking and Unmasking the True Self:
Manipulating Distance in Memoirs and Personal Sketches

WORKSHOP DESCRIPTION

A writer's self is not a given reality but a created resource: You are who you say you are and who you need to be for a particular purpose—as long as you shape this persona to create the desired effect. This creative nonfiction workshop begins by surveying a variety of masked selves in published writing, ranging from intensely intimate to coolly distant. Workshop members then create an inventory of personal traits, following a series of prompts to take a self-inventory of character features; to seek contradictions and usable quirks; to locate interesting conflicts; and to exploit past experiences. Working collaboratively and individually from these raw materials, all choose from a variety of scenarios and writing genres to compose a self-portrait whose controlled perspective reveals an intended, felt truth about oneself. Students will leave with a character sketch of themselves. Intermediate-Level Workshop in Creative Nonfiction:

INSTRUCTOR BIOGRAPHY

Tom Hemmeter is a member of the English Department at Arcadia University, where he directs the Writing Program. He teaches non-fiction writing and film, and he has published academic essays in both areas.

SANDRA HURTES

WRITING YOUR LIFE—THE PERSONAL ESSAY

SUPPLEMENTARY MATERIALS:

ARTICLE: *KEEPING ALIVE THE DREAMS OF LOVE*

Sandra Hurtes
Writing Your Life—The Personal Essay

WORKSHOP DESCRIPTION

In this personal essay writing workshop you'll learn how to mine your life for your richest material. Bring your conflicts, your obsessions, and even your inner critic, if he or she insists on tagging along. This is a hands-on two hours. We'll do writing exercises to access memories and generate essay ideas. You'll gain insight into where your strongest stories are, the elements of a personal essay, and how to work with the material produced in class. Writers at all levels welcome.

INSTRUCTOR BIOGRAPHY

Sandra Hurtes is an essayist and creative writing teacher living in Manhattan. Her work has appeared in *The New York Times*, *The Washington Post*, *Poets & Writers*, *Writer's Digest* and numerous other publications. She received a 2004 award from The American Jewish Press for excellence in Jewish Journalism. Her essays have been anthologized in *Knit Lit the Third* and *The Contemporary Reader and Poetica*. She teaches in continuing education at Hunter College in NYC and in the Special Programs at the University of Pennsylvania.

Word Count: 1250
The New York Times 6/96

Keeping Alive the Dreams of Love
by Sandra Hurtes

It had been a long time since I'd met anyone promising in the romantic arena, and I'd pretty much retired the dreams I'd carried since childhood about marriage and a baby. I'd been settling instead for a sprinkling of dates, here and there, taking what I could get, almost forgetting that I ever wanted more.

One night on a whim I took myself out to a popular Manhattan dance spot where the lights were dim, the music was loud, and the crowd was lively. I sat at a small table surveying the scene when I spotted someone interesting across the dance floor. He looked at me, then looked away, and finally, he held my glance. Before I knew it we were playing the mating and waiting game, until the braver one of us stepped across the great divide and asked, simply, "Would you like to dance?"

We found our way easily into each other's rhythm, and to the tune of, "This Can't Be Love," we covered ground. As we dipped and twirled around the crowded dance floor, he whispered in my ear, "We have great dance compatibility." I heard in his words the hint of a future, and my cautious heart began to come out of hiding.

After dancing a few numbers we stopped to catch our breath, and over drinks we got acquainted. "Do you take lessons?" he asked.

"No, but I'm thinking about it. Maybe West Coast Swing." It seemed like the right thing to say, as if I was in the know. He told me about a new club in Soho, one that he was hoping to try. Then he got down to business. Taking out his wallet he proudly showed me a picture of his son, "From an early marriage," he explained, quickly adding, "It's been over for years." I told him I'd been married once, also long ago, and I had no children. Pushing a ringlet back from my forehead he asked me for my phone number. Then he wrote his own number on a scrap of paper, and his name in case I'd already forgotten. Richard.

We had our first date a week later. It was an easy evening with good conversation in a dark, crowded restaurant. Over shrimp curry and chicken bandore, he told me about his good friend, Carol, who he often went dancing with. She'd recently fallen in love, and he was hoping that would happen for him, too.

"I'd like to get married again and have at least one more child," he said as we walked outside, looking for a cab to send me home in. Standing on the corner not yet ready to part, I felt as if I was dreaming when he said he had told Carol about me. "Let's call her and tell her how our date's going," he said smiling.

When I got home that night I thought about how unusual it was to be with someone who was that open about what he wanted and so eager to involve me in his life. By our second date, his sincerity and lack of pretense were touching me in all the right ways, and my dusty old dreams for marriage and children were tumbling out of the closet.

"It would be nice to have a big family," he said on our third date, "because my parents died when I was so young." My overbearing family seemed heavenly to him. I thought about inviting him for Thanksgiving to show him what the other side was really like. But I held back.

After dinner we went for a walk, and then we stood in front of my apartment building for a long time before he kissed me. As we walked inside we made Plans for our next date. Dancing, we both agreed, at the club in Soho. It had a small dance floor he'd heard. We'd have to go easy on the swirling. Bring it in a little closer.

The next day I thought about what I'd wear on our date and was looking forward to talking to Richard. I didn't hear from him for a few days though, and I thought it was a little odd, since we'd been speaking often. Finally I called him at work but he wasn't there so I left a message. A little impatient, I also left a message on his tape at home. A few days later, still nothing. I was trying hard to keep my mind from going where it wanted to go—he lost interest, I was too eager, he got scared and ran. I found out soon enough it was none of the above.

Three days after our last date, Richard died in his sleep. It wasn't a heart attack, an aneurysm, or anything discernible. The autopsy report that came back eight weeks later was inconclusive but showed that it was of natural causes. I received a phone call from Richard's friend, Carol, exactly a week after our last date. She'd searched his house for my phone number and found it finally on Richard's dresser. She was sorry she didn't get to me sooner, and no, there was nothing I could do. The funeral was already over, and so was *shiva*.

We hung up, and I sat very still waiting to feel something deep and dark inside, something that would move me to cry bitter tears. But I felt nothing. No, I felt eerie. Why, I wondered, through the slow, steady shock that grew heavier not lighter as the days stretched into weeks. Why was I pulled in at the final hours to witness the end of a life I barely knew? What was the reason for us to meet?

Many months later I got my answer. I came home one evening from a date with a man I had started seeing. He was a divorced dad, not looking for a commitment, my usual scenario. As I reviewed my evening with this casual guy, I thought about how disappointed I was that he kept forgetting to show me pictures of his kids, and that he had to cut our night short because there was just too much he had to do the next day. Oh, and about next week, well he didn't know yet if he'd be available. He'd call me.

There was nothing to hope for with this new man, no fantasies to get lost in. It was all pretty dim. That's when I understood why I had to meet Richard. The feelings he stirred in me showed me my desire for love wasn't dead, just buried, and the dreams of my childhood still lingered in anticipation that they might yet come true. No, Richard wasn't taken from me to leave me hungry and wanting. He was given to me to show me the kind of life in which I had stopped believing.

I like to think that there was something special Richard got from me that he took with him to his final sleep. Perhaps he, too, experienced the sweet rush of old dreams resurrected and the wonder of living again in long, forgotten hope. These exquisite treasures so many of us search for and never find, and maybe even worse, some of us no longer look. If that's true for you, then I'm here to tell you. Bringing a heart back to life can sometimes be so simple. For me it all started with a look, a touch, and a dip on the dance floor.

*   *   *

Copyright © 1996 by The New York Times Co. Reprinted with permission.

JESSAMYN JOHNSTON SMYTH

MAKING IT HAPPEN: FROM BLOCK TO BOOK

Jessamyn Johnston Smyth
Making it Happen: From Block to Book

WORKSHOP DESCRIPTION

You've dealt with your blocks and gotten the writing rolling—what happens now? Few programs or classes teach the basic skills every writer needs to get a book into the world. These skills include useful revision strategies and how to get and give truly useful critical feedback, which we'll develop by working on sections of class members' rough drafts. We'll also look at how to choose between traditional and non-traditional publishing options, how to market your work(and when you have to), what marketing really means for writers, how to help each other, and how to use all available resources and technologies to give yourself the best chance of getting your work to your potential readers. Please bring a one-page section of a rough draft of your work. Intermediate to advance level.

INSTRUCTOR BIOGRAPHY

A 2004 Grant Recipient of the Bread Loaf Writer's Conference, **Jessamyn Smyth's** story "A More Perfect Union" has been nominated for The Pushcart Prize. Her book *Koan Garden: Ten Wu Wei Yin Stories* was just released and her award-winning prose and poetry has appeared in numerous print and electronic journals and anthologies. In 2004-2005, Naked Theatre and The Paul Alexander Gallery produced four of her plays, and *The Importance of Being Wild* was the first commissioned work produced by The Shea Theater. Her play *Jenny Haniver* premiered at The Shea Theater's Festival of New Work in March 2006 and was performed again in Vermont in May. Founder and Executive Director of Basilisk, a production company, Jessamyn has taught classes in writing and theater craft at Goddard College, UMASS, and Greenfield Community College. She earned her MFA at Goddard College.

QUINCY SCOTT JONES

SPOKEN WORD, WRITTEN WORD:
PERFORMANCE AND TEXT

SUPPLEMENTARY MATERIALS:

HANDOUT: *PROEM*

Quincy Scott Jones
Spoken Word, Written Word: Performance and Text

WORKSHOP DESCRIPTION

How can a writer demonstrate what is on the page through an oral performance? How can a writer show how much fun his or her piece is? Your work is rich with emotional depth, but does your audience know this? Good work will sell itself, but a good reading helps. This workshop explores the relation between the written piece and the performance of the written piece with a focus on trantioning from textual performance to oral performance. Through various creative writing and theater-inspired exercises, we will work on enunciation, vocal projection, emotional range, body movement/positioning, and other factors that make the difference between a reading and an experience. Want to become a better reader? Bring a three-to-five minute piece to workshop and together we will help you reach your true performance potential.

INSTRUCTOR BIOGRAPHY

Quincy Scott Jones earned a bachelor's degree from Brown University, a master's degree from Temple University, and $100 once working as supermarket clown. He has performed in the Fringe Festival in Philadelphia, Rites & Reason Theatre in Providence, and briefly in the performance group CRQ. He currently he teaches at Temple University and Arcadia University where this Spring he was the instructor for the first ever Poetry on the Page and Stage class.

Proem

Poetic:
the art of writing. In the *Oxford*, stuck between the "podzol," a soil with materials leached from its surface; and "po-faced," humorless. I like this. Poetics: the earth. We are the podzol, the layer just beneath. We smile when we smile, we laugh when we laugh. We are sunrises, and Road Runner cartoons. But underneath: a raindrop, from the skyscraper to the firescape to the canopy. We are the bum we sometimes walk past, sometimes give money to, but always disregard.

Political:
the timely; the New York minute. The awkward seat in the waiting room. The un-round pebble bouncing in the sole. The political; the timely; the New York minute. The "rimed droggle" of abolishment. The Dante; the Shelly; the New York minute. Now Pacifist. Now Communist. Now rapping 'bout myself. The political; the timely; the New York minute.

Pop:
the popular. Britney Spears. Some Blonde Barbie Breast-Implanted Bambino bouncing 'round to bebop beats. Trying to make slavery sound sexy. Slavery was not popular. Spirituals were not popular. Migrations were not popular. Negations were not popular. Segregations were not popular.

> The Blues was not popular.
> Motown was not popular.
> Hip-Hop was not popular.
> Poverty still ain't popular.

And outside the **Pop! Pop!** followed by dead silence. And in this silence, music is made.

Post-pagan:
The Priest-Chief slaps the ceremonial dagger out of my hand.

"We're not doing that anymore.
No more blood, no more pain, no more suffering for the greater good.
No more shrines, no more alters, no more asking if is she's a virgin.
No more rituals, no more dancing, no more stories in the fire.
All stories will now be accepted by email, by the glow of fiber optics,
and the gods, the gods, the gods gotta get jobs.
If you have to pray—I mean have to pray—there's an old man upstairs
reading Neitzsche.
But no more magic; no more miracles; no one cares."

Only Crice can comfort me on a nondescript park bench.
"Its not his fault," she says.
I look up into her faint but easing smile. "Baraka thinks I'm a half-white
college student. I don't think we should see each other anymore."

ELISE JUSKA

VOICE LESSONS: MASTER CLASS

Elise Juska
Voice Lessons: Master Class

WORKSHOP DESCRIPTION

Sarcastic, soothing, loud, bitter, tender, bold—the voice in writing can be as dynamic and revealing as the voice in speaking. In this intense but upbeat workshop, we will pay particular attention to the nature of the written voice as we discuss rough drafts of short stories. Participants will submit their work in advance; instructor will provide detailed written comments. Expect an atmosphere of support, a spirit of discovery, and the fresh perspectives and thorough feedback needed to help take a draft to the next level. Suitable for beginning fiction writers as well as those with fiction writing experience.

INSTRUCTOR BIOGRAPHY

Elise Juska's short stories have appeared in the *Harvard Review, Seattle Review, Calyx, Salmagundi, Black Warrior Review, Philly Fiction, The Hudson Review* (Pushcart Prize nominee) and many other publications. She is the author of the novels *The Hazards of Sleeping Alone* and *Getting Over Jack Wagner,* a Critic's Choice in *People* magazine. Elise teaches fiction writing at the University of the Arts in Philadelphia, the New School in New York City, and the Stonecoast Summer Writers' Conference in Casco Bay, Maine. Her third novel is forthcoming from Simon & Schuster in Summer 2007.

ANNE KAIER

IN THE KITCHEN: LIFE WRITING IN THE RAW

Anne Kaier
In the Kitchen: Life Writing in the Raw

WORKSHOP DESCRIPTION

Whether it's the heart of the home or not, what happens in the kitchen makes for great magazine copy. Maybe you remember your grandfather cooking and telling stories there, maybe you and your kids had royal battles and tender goodbyes there, and maybe you've danced around the kitchen alone on a summer night with an eggbeater for a microphone. The kitchen is where it happens. Learn how to turn your experiences into memorable personal essays. In this course, we will discuss key copy points for the personal essay, write drafts of stories, and talk about possible markets.

INSTRUCTOR BIOGRAPHY

Anne Kaier's articles and reviews have been published in the *Drexel Online Journal*. Her poetry has been published in *Poetry Ink, Bucks County Writer, American Writing, The Schuylkill Valley Journal, Philadelphia Poets* and other magazines as well as online. Her poetry chapbook, InFire, is available from Skintype Press. She participated in *The Kenyon Review* Writers Workshop and has been a Featured Poet at Arcadia University and the Free Library of Philadelphia. She has taught at Harvard, Bryn Mawr College, and the University of Pennsylvania. At Penn State, she teaches courses in article writing. She lives in Center City, Philadelphia and can be reached at AnneKaier@verizon.net.

BILL KENT

PLOTBOILING

SUPPLEMENTARY MATERIALS:

HANDOUT: PLOT BOILING.
OR, WHAT TO DO WHEN NOTHING
HAPPENS NEXT

Bill Kent
Plotboiling

WORKSHOP DESCRIPTION

A story's plot is more than the answer to the question, what happens next. We'll start with a quick overview of basic plot structures, followed by a discussion of the elements of superior plotting: suspenseful pacing, action versus explication, flashbacks, foreshadowing, subplots, red herrings and false climaxes. How else to end, but with endings: happy, sad, circular, surprising, deviously twisted, edge-of-the-seat thrilling and wonderfully strange!

INSTRUCTOR BIOGRAPHY

Bill Kent is a journalist and author of seven novels and two non-fiction books. His journalism has appeared in more than 40 national and regional publications, including the *New York Times*, the *Washington Post* and the *Philadelphia Inquirer*. He has taught journalism and writing at Rutgers and Temple Universities. His most recent novel, *Street Legal*, was published in June by St. Martin's Press.

PLOT BOILING.

OR, WHAT TO DO WHEN NOTHING HAPPENS NEXT

By Bill Kent

Plot is easily defined as what, in a story, emerges from the confusion of what we want to happen, what must happen and what actually happens. Even if the point of the story is that nothing happens, that "nothing" becomes something.

If we accept that storytelling as a zesty blend of character, plot and setting, the process of beginning a story becomes easy. We pick one element over the other two, start with that, and bring the rest in as soon as possible.

If only it were that simple! In truth, stories have at least three beginnings. These can occur in any order, but it's best when they happen rather quickly—simultaneously, if possible.

The first beginning tells us where we are. The second introduces a character about whom we should care. This character may not be the hero or heroine, but he should be important enough so that we can follow this person to The MacGuffin, the third beginning.

The MacGuffin is a term used by Alfred Hitchcock, for the thing, incident or situation that begins the plot. "A MacGuffin is neither relevant, important nor, finally, any of one's business. It simply gets the story going," says Donald Spoto in his biography, *Alfred Hitchcock: the Dark Side of Genius.*

Of course, the MacGuffin can be relevant and important. Like the ear-splitting wail of a fire engine's siren, it gets our attention. What happens after that is everyone's business.

Within the world of fiction are numerous genres—kinds of storytelling—that emphasize different things. The plots of some genres are governed by traditional expectations. A mystery begins with a crime so that, at the end, we expect to learn who committed it and, possibly, get a sense of justice done as the bad guy (or girl) is led away by the police. In a romance, two people are attracted to each other so that, at the end, these people will presumably marry and live happily ever after. In a thriller, the hero is put in peril, or given a difficult, urgent problem on which much depends. We want the hero to turn the tables on his antagonist at the end, and solve the problem.

Other genre plots are less defined. In some character-driven literary novels, the plot is the examination of the hero and the revelation of where he fits into his world. In revenge stories, we follow a heroine's progress as he restores justice by inflicting harm and ruin on those who have done her wrong. The "rites-of-passage" tale, or "bildungsroman" (German for "novel of formation") follows the progress of a young person as he or she grows, matures, suffers the slings and arrows of outrageous misfortune and, by the last page, is better for it. The "strange quest" story, a staple of science fiction and fantasy, requires that our hero, or a group of heroes, embark on a journey through an exotic, dangerous, beautiful but ultimately rewarding landscape, culminating in a final test of character that make the trip worthwhile.

Most literary plots share a common, over-arching structure. They start somewhere, build in intensity with escalating scenes of suspense and excitement culminating in a climax, after which a brief denouement brings us gently back to earth. This plot structure is not universal: Shakespeare followed Hamlet or Macbeth to a decisive action, usually in the middle of the drama. After that, the plays rush to a conclusion as the corpses pile up, culminating in the hero's death.

We also have the point-of-view or Rashomon plot, named for Kurosawa's magnificent whodunnit movie, in which successive retellings of what appear to be the same story lead us to a higher truth.

One last, but certainly not final plot style: the circular plot used in stream-of-consciousness and experimental fiction. Here the story begins at the climax (or near it) and the narrative proceeds with a series of concentric flashbacks that explain to us how we happened to arrive at this point. Then, we get a moment when everything makes sense (or seems to) and the the denouement brings us back to earth.

No matter what the plot structure of your story is, you can be sure that your readers are going to have expectations. If your hero's character is essentially good, that is, pro-social, likeable, sympathetic, readers will want your hero to succeed. If you open your story during the American Civil War, your reader will expect the action to stay in that time and place—and not conclude on a windswept plateau on the Mars in 2947, unless build such possibilities into the narrative.

As artists, we may not want to consider the reader's expectations. We may want to let our story take us where it will. This is a good strategy when we the writing is easy, when events are flowing logically, when we haven't quite figured out our characters and those to whom we've shown our work love it unconditionally.

But those of us who have tried to write a long story have found ourselves in situations in which we run out of gas: when we have no idea hat happens next. Or we want our characters to behave in a way that is unlikely from what has happened so far.

How to proceed? Should we just cling to the formula, and fulfill traditional expectations in the hope that our story will be better received, or more easily published? Certainly not!

Instead, consider some general strategies.

1. Let yourself get even deeper into the world of your story. Let the characters show you what they want to do. Or, look for inspiration in the setting. Examine it more thoroughly, either through research, observation, or that most vital quality of all: imagination.

2. If you want your character to demonstrate a talent or skill at a decisive moment, go back to the beginning of the narrative and mention this skill, or foreshadow it in some way.

3. "Unlikely" is a matter of how much, or how little, you've shown your reader the world of your book. Consider that one reason that art is so necessary is that reality just isn't good enough, or, it isn't as good as it could be. Art gives us something we can't get anywhere else. So, don't be afraid to make what in this world is unlikely, necessary in the world of your story.

4. Avoid the gratuitous: scenes of sex, violence, consumption or venality that you feel are required to make your story more appealing to readers.

5. You create suspense when your reader cares about what happens to the characters. What the reader cares about has a great deal to do with what you care about. If you've run out of gas, ask yourself what's most interesting about your characters. Go back to that, even if the result is making some changes.

6. When in doubt about the plot, ask yourself what the reader might expect should happen here. Then, give yourself a choice. You can either grant the reader's expectations in your own original way, or provide something even better. When this better thing becomes an unusually delightful surprise, this is called a "plot twist."

7. Limit your flashbacks because they tend to slow the narrative momentum. If you think it's very important that we get a glimpse of the villain's terrible childhood, indulge yourself and put it in. But don't be afraid to take it out if it becomes a distraction.

8. The climax doesn't have to be the logical culmination of the events in the narrative. Its function is to release tension by either settling the score or giving specific characters exactly what they deserve.

9. Finish the story before revising it. When you've reached an ending, you have a better idea of what fits and what doesn't.

10. A good test for deciding whether a passage or scene should stay or go. Ask two questions. Does this reveal character? Does this further the plot? If yes to either, it stays. If no, remove it (save it in a file in your word processor) and see if the patient lives. You can always put it back in if you don't like the final result.

> To practice any art, no matter how well or badly, is a way to make your soul grow. So do it.
>
> —Kurt Vonnegut

(end)

DAVE KOCH

AUTHENTICATING DETAILS IN LITERARY FICTION (ADVANCED)

Dave Koch
Authenticating Details In Literary Fiction (Advanced)

WORKSHOP DESCRIPTION

"I want to know more" is the most common (and least helpful) of the old saw workshop comments, the sort of things new writers hear over and over and then over again. This lecture will address using authenticating details in literary fiction to capture what's being described in a way that'll leave readers (and fellow workshop participants) feeling like they know just enough. Topics will include descriptive lies that get at the truth and how authenticating details allow the reader to do his own work.

INSTRUCTOR BIOGRAPHY

Dave Koch currently teaches fiction writing at the Gotham Writers Workshop in Manhattan, and recently finished a stint as a Visiting Professor of Creative Writing at St. Vincent College in Pennsylvania. He's a founding editor of the Land-Grant College Review.

DIANA LAMBERT

POINT OF VIEW—
MAKING AN INFORMED CHOICE

Diana Lambert
Point of View—Making an Informed Choice.

WORKSHOP DESCRIPTION

"Harry stepped into the rain."

"I step into the rain and shiver."

"Many years ago, never mind how long ago precisely, I stepped into the rain."

"Harry stepped into the rain and looked up into the sky. Mabel saw Harry gazing into the sky and thought how cute he looked."

Did you ever stop to think why you were choosing a particular point of view for your story? How do you know how to tell your story? What point of view do you use? How does point of view affect your whole story? In this course, we will start out with a brief overview of all the point of view choices at your disposal. Then we'll look at some well-known fiction to see how the point-of-view works and why the author made the choices he/she did. Finally, through a series of in-class exercises, you'll revise the same story using several different points of view. Level: Beginner to Intermediate

INSTRUCTOR BIOGRAPHY

Diana Lambert earned her MFA from Warren Wilson College. Her work has appeared in such magazines as *ACM: Another Chicago Magazine* and *Columbia*. She is a recent finalist of the Dana Award in Short Fiction as well as the Novel, and teaches fiction and expository writing at several community colleges.

MARC LAPADULA

THINKING IN PICTURES: WRITING YOUR MOVIE IDEA, PART 1 (SCREENWRITING I)

THINKING IN PICTURES: WRITING YOUR MOVIE IDEA, PART 2 (SCREENWRITING II)

Marc Lapadula
**Thinking in Pictures: Writing Your Movie Idea,
Part 1 (Screenwriting I)**

**Thinking in Pictures: Writing Your Movie Idea,
Part 2 (Screenwriting II)**

WORKSHOP DESCRIPTION

Part 1:

This two-part workshop looks at the screenplay as both a literary text and blueprint for production. We will critically analyze several classic screenplay texts such as *Rebel Without a Cause*, and *Psycho*, focusing on character enhancement, creating "believable" cinematic dialogue, plot development and story structure, conflict, pacing, dramatic foreshadowing, the element of surprise, text and subtext, and visual story-telling. *Please make sure you watch both movies in advance.*

The instructor will have available, for a discounted price of $35, a course pack including relevant material and one screenplay.

Part 2:
See "Thinking in Pictures: Writing Your Movie Idea, Part 1 (Screenwriting I)" held on Sunday, October 15, 10:00am-12:00pm)

INSTRUCTOR BIOGRAPHY

Marc Lapadula holds an MFA from the Iowa Writers Workshop and is a screenwriter/playwright who runs the screenwriting program at Yale University. He also lectures at PENN, Johns Hopkins and Columbia University's Graduate Film School. He has consulted for several studios and independent producers and has had several screenplays commissioned and optioned. Among them: *Distant Influence, Loner,*

Night Bloom and an adaptation of Mikhail Bulgalkov's *Heart of a Dog*. His published play, *Dancer*, was produced in the Samuel French Festival in New York. He also produced *Angel Passing*, starring Hume Cronyn, which premiered at the Sundance Film Festival and most recently co-produced *Mentor*, starring Rutger Hauer which premiered at the 2006 Tribeca Film Festival.

His former students have won many grand prizes in national contests (Nicholl, Chesterfield, Disney, Austin, Expo 4, etc.) and have sold scripts that have been produced (i.e. *The Breakup* and the *Cry Wolf*). They also write for several TV shows (i.e., *Law and Order, Family Guy, The Agency, Highlander, SCRUBS* and others).

MOLLY LAYTON

FICTIONAL TECHNIQUES IN NONFICTION

Molly Layton
Fictional Techniques in Nonfiction

WORKSHOP DESCRIPTION

Whether in memoirs or other essays, writers set up specific scenes, summon characters, and even engage these characters in dialogue. But when do these and other mainstays of fiction hinder rather than help the power and depth of the writer's explorations? In this workshop we will talk about the special trance of fiction and contrast that with the peculiar opportunities in creative nonfiction. Be prepared to write a little and read a little.

INSTRUCTOR BIOGRAPHY

Molly Layton is a psychologist in private practice and the recipient of a 2003 Leeway Foundation award for fiction and creative nonfiction. Her essay about James Frey, "Telling Stories," appeared in the July *Psychotherapy Networker*. Three other essays appear in *The Best of the Networker: Our All-Time Top 10 Articles*. A short story, *Senseless*, was nominated for a Pushcart Prize.

FRED LEEBRON

INHABITING POINT OF VIEW

Fred Leebron
Inhabiting Point of View

WORKSHOP DESCRIPTION

This workshop will examine a primary strategy in creating successful fiction, invoking the concept of the writer as medium through which the characters speak and act. The outline for the two hour session includes a discussion of various models for reading and writing fiction, an investigation of how creating character arcs can entail all elements of fiction writing, and a consideration of various strategies writers might take to inhabit their characters and thereby create transportive and resonant work

INSTRUCTOR BIOGRAPHY

Fred Leebron was founding director of the Fine Arts Work Center in Provincetown's Summer Program of Workshops and Residencies. Currently he is a Professor of English at Gettysburg College and the Program Director of the M.F.A. in Creative Writing at Queens University of Charlotte. Fred's novels include *Six Figures, Out West*, and *In the Middle of All This*, and he is co-author of *Creating Fiction: A Writer's Companion* and co-editor of *Postmodern American Fiction: A Norton Anthology*. Awards for his writing include a Wallace Stegner Fellowship, a Fulbright Scholarship, an O. Henry Award, and a Pushcart Prize. The Canadian production of *Six Figures* premiered at the 2005 Toronto Film Festival and was a nominee for a Genie (a Canadian Oscar) for best adapted screenplay. Fred's essays and stories appear frequently in magazines such as *Tin House, Redbook, Grand Street, Parenting, Threepenny Review, More*, and *Ploughshares*.

JONATHAN MABERRY

CAREERS IN WRITING

Jonathan Maberry
Careers In Writing

WORKSHOP DESCRIPTION

Do you want to write but don't know how to go about it? Do you want to make money as a writer? You may already have the skills necessary to break into one of the many writing-related fields. Award-winning author, book doctor and writing career counselor Jonathan Maberry presents a fun, faced-paced and deeply informative program on Careers in Writing. The workshops covers topics such as: Breaking into the magazine market (the easy way); starting (and finishing) a novel; How to find an agent; small jobs and quick $$ for writers; managing a part-time writing career while working a full-time job; finding the right markets for your writing; discovering what kind of writer you are, and much more! Your writing career might be within reach. (Grab for it!)

INSTRUCTOR BIOGRAPHY

Jonathan Maberry is a professional writer and writing teacher; since 1979 he's sold more than 900 articles, sixteen nonfiction books, three novels, as well as short stories, poetry, song lyrics, video scripts, and two plays. Pinnacle Books will release his thriller novel, *Ghost Road Blues*, in 2006, to be followed by two sequels in 2007 and 2008. In September 2006 Citadel Books will release *Vampire Universe: The Dark World of Supernatural Beings That Hunt Us, Haunt Us and Hunger For Us*, the first of a series of four nonfiction books of supernatural folklore. He is executive director of The Career Doctor for Writers (*www.careerdoctorforwriters.com*), which provides workshops, classes and editorial services for writers of all genres, is on the board of the Philadelphia Writers, is a member of the Mystery Writers of America, and is president of the NJ-PA Chapter of the Horror Writers

Association. He teaches both fiction and nonfiction, and frequently lectures at writers' conferences how to break into the writing business. Co-founder and co-executive editor of *The Wild River Review*, an online literary magazine (*www.wildriverreview.com*), in April 2006, Jonathan opened The Writers Corner in Doylestown, PA (*www.writerscornerusa.com*), in partnership with writers Brian O'Connell and Joy Stocke. The Writers Corner provides workshops on the craft and business of writing.

SUSAN MAGEE

HOW TO WRITE A TERRIFIC NON-FICTION BOOK PROPOSAL

Susan Magee
How To Write A Terrific Non-Fiction Book Proposal

WORKSHOP DESCRIPTION

To get an agent and to sell a non-fiction book, you don't need a finished manuscript; you need a terrific book proposal. Using real-life examples of successful book proposals that sold, we'll discuss the seven key ingredients of book proposals, including the single most important thing you need to do to sell your proposal to a publisher in today's super competitive market. Next, we'll look at real-life contracts, and then discuss agents, advances, and what you need to know about collaborations. So bring your good idea for a book plus a serious desire to publish, and this class will get you started.

INSTRUCTOR BIOGRAPHY

Susan Magee is the author/co-author of over seven non-fiction books, including *The Jerk With The Cell Phone*, which was featured on CNN and 20/20. Her newest book, *The Pregnancy Countdown Book*, was recently published by Quirk Books. Susan is the former director of publicity for Running Press Book Publishers. She has done freelance PR and copywriting in the publishing industry for over 10 years. Susan holds an MFA in creative writing and literature from Bennington College. Her short stories have won several awards, including the Pennsylvania Council on the Arts and two Leeway Foundation awards.

JANICE MERENDINO

SEE WHAT YOU WANT TO SAY:
DRAWING FOR WRITERS

SUPPLEMENTARY MATERIALS:

HANDOUT: WORKSHOP NOTES

Janice Merendino
See What You Want to Say: Drawing for Writers

WORKSHOP DESCRIPTION

Absolutely no art skills are required, in fact the worse your stick figures are, the better! Learn to "Branch Out" with drawing exercises that are a lot of fun and specifically designed for the non-artist. Drawing prepares you to observe fine distinctions and understand the nuances of what you see. Add this tool to your set of skills and you will have more ways to "envision" something, learn about it and communicate it more clearly. You will enhance your ability to think in images and visually consider composition, structure, metaphors and narrative.

INSTRUCTOR BIOGRAPHY

Janice Merendino is a member of the faculty of Rosemont College's Fine Arts division and teaches in the Masters of English and Publishing program. She is the Director of the Branch Out Project (*www.branchoutproject.com*), an organization that gives visual literacy workshops for major corporations, government agencies, schools and community groups. In addition, Janice has co-authored two articles on using the arts to stimulate creative thinking in law practices.

Workshop Notes—*See What You Want to Say: Drawing for Writers*
Presenter: Janice Merendino
www.branchoutproject.com

I.   Visual Literacy: Why Everyone Should Learn to Draw

Visual literacy is the ability to "read" and find meaning in the visual forms of objects, movements, and symbols and the capacity to create visual forms that carry meaning. This language of image can often communicate what is difficult to express in words. It brings a new "vocabulary" to bear on the information we receive so that we approach our own work with a broader understanding of its meaning and effects.

Developing visual literacy helps us connect with others and think for ourselves. We learn to trust our ability to make fine distinctions and understand the nuances of what we see, what is said and how it's received. This makes us less likely to let others interpret the world for us or manipulate us in ways that are not in our best interest.

Drawing is the best way to acquire visual literacy. Embedded in the drawing process are problem-solving skills that can impact people's lives at home and at work. By giving non-artists the training normally reserved for artists we break the cycle of habitual thinking and gain creative problem-solving skills that can be directly applied to other disciplines. This gives us new ways to do business, educate our children and look more critically at existing bodies of knowledge.

Learning to draw produces a change in attitude that affects other areas of our lives. When beginners are able to produce satisfying results using ideas and techniques usually thought of as advanced, their confidence and desire for mastery increases. As they identify other self-imposed constraints, they discover more of who they are and expand their ideas of what is possible. In addition, apart from developing drawing skills, the Branch Out Project exercises can help participants become more creative in other areas of their lives by encouraging them to identify and break through assumptions, see more options, and recognize the consequences of exercising those options. Specifically, they learn that:

- problem situations can be viewed as compositions or systems that are made up of interdependent pieces in which everything affects everything else.
- the relationships between these pieces are fluid, and it is possible and often preferable to rearrange them.
- each object or situation can be interpreted from many perspectives, and each interpretation has a set of assumptions bound to it.
- a clearer picture of a situation can be created by thinking abstractly, using analogy and metaphor to deepen understanding.

It is important to note that you do not have to be able to draw well to gain this understanding. It is the process of learning that allows you to see things differently and apply these skills. In fact, beginners often have the freshest insights.

II. Why Should Writers Learn to Draw?

Although The Branch Out Project is not a writing course, it can stimulate the thinking of writers by introducing metaphors and concepts that are useful to them in their writing. Specifically, learning to draw gives writers tools to:

- observe and describe the world,
- represent the "inside world", emotions and the inner state of characters,
- eliminate mixed messages in their writing and produce more focused communication, and
- think about structure and address writing problems.

Tools to observe and describe the world

Although both words and images are used to describe the world, they do so in radically different ways. When the brain scans an image, there is no set path for the eye to follow (though the visual artist does try to influence the path the viewer's eye will take). The image is perceived as a whole, all over at once. When reading words, the eye moves linearly along a set path. Meaning unfolds in time as the reader is presented with a part of the "picture", guesses about the rest, and then has those guesses confirmed or confounded by the words that follow. This makes writing well suited to experiences that unfold in time, and images suited to more static scenes. Because writers need to convey both static and dynamic experiences to readers, they must develop their ability to present an image in words. Learning to draw offers a way to do this. When you learn to draw you learn a new way to make observations. These observations can be a gross understanding of what something looks or feels like or a more refined and detailed idea of what you see.

By learning how an artist makes observations and creates an image, writers can use their own images as a basis for their writing. For example, education authority Janet Olson has shown that children who first draw a picture related to their narrative write with much more detail and coherence than students who didn't. In addition, a number of successful authors use visual images, either as inspiration or as a way to organize and structure their narratives.

Tools to represent the "inside world"

Emotions and psychological states are often difficult to convey because they are abstract, they can be stated to the reader but not seen. Non-verbal languages can often communicate what is difficult express in words. For example, body language can effectively convey the psychological state of a character through gesture and posture. When writers practice reading and drawing these gestures they build a new "vocabulary" for this language that can be incorporated into their writing. Drawing exercises for writers can include practicing ways to visually represent emotions as abstract images and then discussing their insights with others.

Tools to eliminate mixed messages and produce more focused communication

In everyday life, we extract meaning from situations by using both visual and narrative approaches. In addition to the words being used, the environment in which the message takes place and the tone of voice and/or body language of the messenger help to deliver meaning and set expectations. When the verbal and non-verbal messages are consistent and reinforce a particular view, the acceptance and overall impact of that view is increased. When they are not consistent, we are less able to extract a clear meaning and it can cause confusion. This is important to writers because readers create images in their own mind to compliment the words they read on the page. To the extent that writers can influence these images, they can influence how their work is interpreted. As writers learn to create visual images they are in a better position to see the possible interpretations and potential confusion that readers may hold in their minds.

Tools to think about structure and address writing problems

The tools to help writers think about structure are indirect but nonetheless valuable. Writers are encouraged to pay attention to the way they draw and to identify those problems that are most similar to the problems they face in crafting a written work.

For example, in drawing a still life of several objects, the temptation is to work object by object, completing each one before moving on to the next. One may have the idea that if each object is drawn well, then the entire drawing will be perfect. But as your technical skills develop, so does your ability to see more clearly. By the time you begin to draw your second or third object, it becomes embarrassingly clear that the first object wasn't drawn accurately. Rather than start over, you decide that it's easier to adjust the second object to make the first object look better. This adjusting "snowballs" until the entire drawing is distorted with a series of compensations based on an earlier flawed decision. Even with new information pointing to something we missed, we seem to fear failure so much (in this case the dread of starting over) that we end up perpetuating our mistakes—a sort of sunk-cost bias.

Another common drawing problem is limiting your options for a solution by perceiving a single cause and consequently, defining the problem too narrowly. For example, struggling unsuccessfully to fix something in your drawing, you discover that the problem lies somewhere else entirely. This is an example of trying to understand the whole by analyzing each of the parts separately. A major shift in thinking occurs when you understand the relationship of the parts to the whole.

The solution to both of these drawing problems is to not focus on completing one object at a time, but instead to "skip around", constantly checking one part of the drawing in relation to another. It is as if you are looking through a camera and bringing the entire subject into focus at the same time.

My hope is that writers empowered with visual literacy skills will come to more fully express themselves, better understand their own motivations and those of others, and to contribute to the world with more enthusiasm, depth, and compassion.

ANNE E. MICHAEL

ENVIRONMENT AS LITERATURE

Anne E. Michael
Environment as Literature

WORKSHOP DESCRIPTION

Gretel Ehrlich, Terry Tempest Williams, Barry Lopez, John McPhee—many of today's CNF writers are finding inspiration and success in the broad arena of environmentalism. Fiction writers and a growing number of poets also work extensively with the many possible themes ecological awareness presents. If your writing touches on topics from outdoorsmanship to gardening to monkeywrenching activism (and anything in between), you may be working the eco-lit genre. In this seminar, we'll discuss ways to get your work into print: which publications are using environmentally-themed literature, how to market such pieces for more general-audience publications, and what constitutes "eco-criticism." We'll also learn how to find like-minded authors, editors, and websites, and what risks one takes when publishing environmental literature. Whether your environment is as big as the Pacific Ocean or as small as a balcony garden, you might be surprised at the breadth of the market for this work.

INSTRUCTOR BIOGRAPHY

Ann E. Michael (*www.annemichael.com*) writes poems and essays from her "rur-burbian" home in Pennsylvania, where she lives with her husband, two children, and numerous pets. Her work has been published in many journals, including *Poem, 9th Letter, The Writer's Chronicle, ISLE, Natural Bridge, Runes*, and others. She is a past recipient of a Pennsylvania Council on the Arts Fellowship in Poetry. Her chapbooks include *More than Shelter*, published by Spire Press, *Small Things Rise & Go*, from FootHills Publishing, and *The Minor Fauna*, from Finishing Line Press. Her CNF pieces on topics artistic, poetic, scientific, and environmental are appearing in journals such as *ISLE, Isotope*, and *Diner*.

JEN MILLER

CORPORATE WRITING FOR CREATIVE PEOPLE

Jen Miller
Corporate Writing for Creative People

WORKSHOP DESCRIPTION

It would be lovely if every freelance writer spent her days writing beautiful profiles, creative narratives or hunting down sources and quotes for that next long form journalism gem. Unfortunately, that's rarely the case, so I propose a session that will show writers how to supplement their incomes by doing what they do best: writing, but for organizations. The opportunities are out there, and they're not all boring, whether it's writing press releases for a university, marketing brochures for an economic development committee or text for a pharmaceutical company website. The course will teach you to identify who might use freelancers, who to approach at companies, how to turn their journalism clips into marketing materials, what to charge, and where to network. I will also discuss the ethical complications that come with writing for organizations and explain why you can't write about and for the same organization.

INSTRUCTOR BIOGRAPHY

Jen Miller is a freelance writer who has worked as an editor and journalist since 2002. As editor of *SJ Magazine*, she ran the publication from top to bottom, from creative brainstorming to assigning articles to editing freelance assignments to final publication. She has recently been a full-time freelancer for publications that include *The New York Times*, *The Philadelphia Inquirer*, *Wired*, *Health*, *USAirways Magazine*, *New Jersey Monthly* and *Pages*. She also writes website text and newsletters for corporate clients. She has taught writing at Camden County Community College and has been a guest lecturer in writing at Rutgers University Camden.

JUDITH MOFFET

SCIENCE FICTION AND FANTASY

Judith Moffet
Science Fiction and Fantasy

WORKSHOP DESCRIPTION

What is science fiction? How does it differ from fantasy, and what distinguishes both from "mainstream" fiction? Where do writers get the ideas for their stories? How is writing for a print market different from writing a script for an "Enterprise" episode? Part lecture, part discussion, part writing exercise, part question-and-answer, this course will address all these issues and others you bring with you.

INSTRUCTOR BIOGRAPHY

Judith Moffett taught creative writing at the Iowa Writers' Workshop and for many years at the University of Pennsylvania. The author of ten books in five genres, including three science-fiction novels and a story collection, she divides her time between Swarthmore PA and her farm in Lawrenceburg KY.

NICK MONTFORT

INTO THE MYST:
WRITING INTERACTIVE FICTION

SUPPLEMENTARY MATERIALS:

EXCERPT: *BOOK AND VOLUME*

Nick Montfort
Into The Myst: Writing Interactive Fiction

WORKSHOP DESCRIPTION

This course covers the basics of writing interactive fiction. After Adventure (also called Colossal Cave) was developed more than 30 years ago, works of interactive fiction (also known as text adventures) became some of the best-selling pieces of entertainment software of the 1980s. Now, free and powerful development systems are available to anyone, and they provide one of the most advanced "writerly" ways to create interactive experiences on the computer, experiences that can be both literary and transformative. We will discuss some successful examples of interactive fiction, look at the elements of the form and the fundamentals of designing and writing works of this sort, and dive into the development process by modifying an existing work. Writing interactive fiction is an enjoyable pursuit for its own sake. It can also help writers work toward designing or writing for commercial computer games, and can provide a better understanding of how computing and writing can fit together.

INSTRUCTOR BIOGRAPHY

Nick Montfort is an interactive fiction author whose releases include *Book and Volume* (2005), *Ad Verbum* (2000), and *Winchester's Nightmare* (1999). He wrote the book *Twisty Little Passages: An Approach to Interactive Fiction* (MIT Press, 2003) and co-edited *The New Media Reader* (MIT Press, 2003). He is also poet, has collaborated on many digital literary projects of different sorts, and is vice president of the Electronic Literature Organization, which can be found online at eliterature.org. Nick is completing a Ph.D. in computer and information science at Penn. His research deals with adding narrative variation to interactive fiction. Nick writes regularly at the group blog *Grand Text Auto*, grandtextauto.org. His interactive fiction and other writing projects he has done for the computer are available at his site, *nickm.com*.

This introduction is taken from Nick Montfort's 2005 interactive fiction **Book and Volume**. *It describes conventions and ways of interacting that have been standard in interactive fiction for decades.*

An Introduction to Interactive Fiction

Interactive fiction provides a world, complete with a setting that is a simulated space, objects and characters that exist within that space, and even unusual physical laws.

This world and the things that happen in it are described to you, the player, in text. You control a character, the "player character," by typing short commands that express what you want the character to do next. Many simple commands that you could give to an actor, standing on stage with the appropriate props around, should be understood.

The ">" prompt is what indicates that it's your turn to type something, for instance:

>OPEN THE CD CASE
>PURCHASE A WIDGET
>ASK THE GOON FOR THE TIME

The first of these is only a sensible command when there is a CD case in the player character's possession or in the area; the second can only be expected to work if the player character has money and is somewhere where widgets are sold; and the last command will only be meaningful if there is a goon nearby or otherwise available for communication.

Headings, shown in bold, indicate the current location of the player character. The current location is also named in the upper right; the obvious ways to leave are indicated in the upper left. The command EXITS will result in the obvious ways to leave being named explicitly.

Upon entering a location, the area will be described. To take a closer look at something in the location or in the player character's possession, you can EXAMINE or LOOK AT it. In *Book and Volume*, the first description may provide more commentary or reminisces than later descriptions.

You can command the player character to manipulate things in the world, too: to pick up certain things, turn some devices on and off, and eat food, for instance. The player character can also be commanded to talk to some other characters.

SCORE and FULL SCORE provide some information about how you are progressing at some tasks.

First-time players are sometimes frustrated that certain commands will not work, but there is some sort of system to interactive fiction. The sort of commands that usually don't work include:

[No . . .] >DONATE MY ORGANS TO SCIENCE

Unless the player character has just been presented with a blank organ donor card, there would be no obvious way to do this. Even in that case, something more specific and concrete, such as CHECK THE TOP BOX, might be more effective. Commands should generally have something to do with concrete things in the immediate area, although conversations with other characters might be about abstract topics.

[No . . .] >GO TO TANGIERS

The player character is usually only able to move around locally, following such commands as GO NORTH, LEAVE, and GO TO THE RESTAURANT (when there is a single restaurant in the immediate area). An indicator in the upper left shows what directions the player character can move in. You can also type EXITS to see these directions listed.

More generally, complex actions that involve numerous steps (purchasing a plane ticket, booking a hotel room, packing for a trip, arranging ground transportation to the airport, waiting in line at security, and so on) cannot usually be accomplished with a single command. Some actions of moderate complexity might be possible with single commands, however, if they are routine ones for the player character.

[No . . .] >WALK TO THE COFFEE TABLE

If there's a coffee table in the room, you can just directly command the player character to do several things: look at it, take things off it, put things on it, and so forth. There's usually no need to move the player character around in front of specific pieces of furniture; just specifying what is to be done is enough.

[No . . .] >SLYLY SPRYLY RUN

One problem is that the command does not specify where to run to or what direction to run in. Also, the adverbs will not be understood. Generally, adverbs are unnecessary. You are asked to choose what basic things the player character does, not the very fine details of how those actions are accomplished.

You may want to take some notes as you play interactive fiction. Traditionally, players have drawn a map as they progress through a particular interactive fiction world; this may or may not be necessary for particular people playing particular pieces of interactive fiction.

Finally, playing interactive fiction with others, in person or online, is probably the best introduction. Even if your fellow players are not interactive fiction experts, different people will have different good ideas about how to make progress, and working together can be fun.

An Example Transcript

Nick Montfort's Ad Verbum *presents the text adventurer with puzzles that are logological in nature, from the realm of recreational linguistics, or wordplay. The situation is a parody of the stereotypical treasure hunt. To solve the puzzles of* Ad Verbum, *however, it's necessary to discover the scheme of writing that is being used and to imitate that scheme when typing in commands. Although* Ad Verbum *is unusual in this way, the basic ways of getting around the environment and the possibilities for commanding the main character are similar to those in other interactive fiction.*

With the cantankerous Wizard of Wordplay evicted from his mansion, the worthless plot can now be redeveloped. The city regulations declare, however, that the rip-down job can't proceed until all the items within have been removed. That's what the demolition contractor explains to you, anyway, as you stand eagerly on the adventurer's day labor corner. Once he learns of your penchant for puzzle-solving and your kleptomaniacal tendencies, he hires you for the job. You hop into the bed of his truck, type a few Zs, and arrive at the site, eager

. . .

AD VERBUM

By & (C) 2000 Nick Montfort <*nickm@nickm.com*>
Please type the words and read the PREFACE, WARNING, and LICENSE.
Release 4 / Serial number 010803 / Inform v6.21 Library 6/10

Foyer
    This is the mansion's spacious ground-floor antechamber. The wallpaper is peeling and bits of plaster have fallen from the ceiling here and there. There is a stairway, stable enough to ascend. The big area to the west must have once been a separate room, but the demolition crew seems to have already taken out a wall. A living room is east. On the south side is the front door. A Dumpster has been dumped here.
    The contractor clears his throat and points at the big Dumpster. "Forget the fixtures, but pick up everything that's not bolted down, including the stuff out back. Then, drop off all the debris—er, I mean, um, treasures—right here . . ." He scrawls something on the Dumpster with a marker. "Good luck!" The contractor hurries out the front door, which slams closed, leaving you alone.
    You spot a door to the north, leading out back. It is shut quite tight.
    >examine the dumpster
    It's made of steel, and almost entirely open on one end for easy deposition of debris. Scrawled across it is the phrase "ATROPHY CASE." Perhaps the contractor left out a space when labelling it.
    >preface

. . .

>warning

. . .

>climb the stairs

Initial Lobby

The lobby of the mansion's initial floor—the one above the ground floor—is an ordinary and fairly well-maintained room. There are some things scrawled on the ground here, in the contractor's handwriting: '1 object' is written to the north, while toward the other three exits on this floor '2' is scrawled. The stairway that runs down to the foyer turns and continues up, to the next floor. The constrained passages to the north, east, west, and south look as if they might spell trouble. Or perhaps they simply spell 'NEWS.'

>south

"LISTEN WELL!" a sonorous voice booms out, in attempted hollowness. "Know ye that passage back through here is difficult for some, impossible for others! Should you wish to transport yourself—without your cherished possessions—out of these constrained confines, utter the magic command: START!"

Sloppy Salon

Simple social space, sadly spoiled. Some skewed situation's sequel, surely. Seemingly, slovenly students sojourned—scraping, scratching, scuffing surfaces.

Stuff: . . . stainless steel stapler . . . sizable sofa.

>take stapler

Stop! Stop! Show some sense. Scribble suitable strings.

>get stapler

Stop! Stop! Sinful speech. Select superior symbols.

>steal stapler

Seized.

[+2.]

>steal sofa

Sizable sofa sits solidly, stubborn.

>south

Sorry. Structural surroundings stop southern striding.
>saunter
Sure. Simply say such, specifically.
>split

Initial Lobby

The lobby of the mansion's initial floor—the one above the ground floor—is an ordinary and fairly well-maintained room. There are some things scrawled on the ground here, in the contractor's handwriting: '1 object' is written to the north, while toward the other three exits on this floor '2' is scrawled. The stairway that runs down to the foyer turns and continues up, to the next floor. The constrained passages to the north, east, west, and south look as if they might spell trouble. Or perhaps they simply spell 'NEWS.'

[+3.]
>up

Antepenultimate Lobby

This lobby, allowing access to the rooms of the next-to-next-to-top floor, is in good shape. It is very similar to the lobby below, although the ceiling may be a bit lower. Here there are only three passages. Two of them (to the north and east) are normal passages, but one, to the south, is oddly constrained. It has an ominous sign above it. The main stairway leads down, while another staircase, straight and narrow, allows passage up to the next floor.

>up

Penultimate Lobby

At this level the house is neither as broad or as long as it is on the ground floor. There seems to only be one other room on this floor, through a constrained double doorway to the west. One thin, unpainted stairway leads up into darkness from here. Another one, almost as narrow, leads down.

>go west

You'll never get through those constrained double doors carrying that stainless steel stapler.

>drop the stapler

Dropped.

>go west

"LISTEN WELL!" a sonorous voice booms out, in attempted hollowness. "Know ye that passage back through here is difficult for some, impossible for others! Should you wish to transport yourself—without your cherished possessions—out of these constrained confines, utter the magic command: APPROACH THE APPROACH!"

Twin Bedroom

This is a reasonably-sized bedroom, laid out symmetrically. On the room's centerline is a scan of two photographs, framed and affixed to the wall. A double doorway, now bereft of doors but clearly marked "EXIT," leads out, to the east.

Fortunately, someone's already cleared out the twin beds.

(The mansion, incidentally, like many adventure game houses, seems rather inadequately supplied with bathrooms. Perhaps there are certain adventurer functions that are better elided, though.)

Your object-sensitive eyes notice: . . . pile of feed.

>take the feed

Type the type of thing that is permitted here.

>examine the scan

Type the type of thing that is permitted here.

>scan the scan

The scan of the two photographs is set in a frame that is actually nailed to the wall. This is too bad, because of course you would like to take this object. But since it is fixed to the structure, it means the job of getting it downstairs falls to someone else.

The photo on the left side of the scan is of a famous cello player: Yo Yo Ma. The photo on the right depicts a man standing behind a United Nations podium. It's Boutros Boutros Ghali.

###

Ad Verbum is available online at: *http://nickm.com/if/adverbum.html*

Book and Volume is available at: *http://nickm.com/if/book_and_volume.html*

JACK MURNIGHAN

HOW TO WRITE A GREAT SEX SCENE

Jack Murnighan
How to Write a Great Sex Scene

WORKSHOP DESCRIPTION

This is a how-to course in the elements of quality erotic fiction and
non-fiction. There won't be time to demonstrate how to write full-on
erotica, but I'll show you how to get started or how to add a sexual
component to a pre-existing work. Too often, at a potentially steamy
(and often emotionally and psychologically critical) juncture in a
story, authors, instead of actually describing what happens, insert a
paragraph break and tpe the word "Afterwards." If you'd like to avoid
this cop-out and actually be able to make the narrative most of bodies
(and their requisite minds) colliding, this course will help. I will bring
readings to class, but students are also encouraged to send samples of
their work for discussion. Email me at *ondemandediting@gmail.com*

INSTRUCTOR BIOGRAPHY

Jack Murnighan teaches freelance writing at The University of the
Arts. He is the former editor of Nerve.com (four time Webby award-
winner), has had stories published in *The Best American Erotica* series
three times, co-edited a collected called *Full Frontal Fiction*, and has
published two books on sex in the history of literature: *The Naughty
Bits* and *Classic Nasty*. He also writes for the glossies and will be the
sex and relationship advice columnist for a new national women's
magazine launching this Fall. He lives in New York City.

DANIEL NESTER

GENRE IN DRAG: THE EXPERIMENTAL ESSAY

Daniel Nester
Genre in Drag: The Experimental Essay

WORKSHOP DESCRIPTION

The essay gets a bad rap these days. It's often the five-paragraph grunt work of exams or applications. However, the essay, in its purest form, is the exploration of an idea, no matter how many paragraphs or diversions—stylistic or rhetorical—it takes. The word essay itself comes from the old French essai, which means "to try," and the Latin exagium, "to weigh or evaluate." As Montaigne, the father of the personal essay, writes, "Let attention be paid not to the matter, but to the shape I give it." In this class, we will look at some of those different shapes experimental essays have taken over the years. We will also start and put together a couple experimental essays of our own: We'll write lists together, set up a form, give each other assignments. northern panhandle and is currently working on a second collection of short fiction.

INSTRUCTOR BIOGRAPHY

Daniel Nester is the author of *God Save My Queen* (Soft Skull Press, 2003) and *God Save My Queen II* (2004), both lyric essay collections on his obsession with the rock band Queen, as well as *The History of My World Tonight* (BlazeVox, 2006). His writing has appeared in *Mr. Beller's Neighborhood, Creative Nonfiction, Poets & Writers, Time Out New York*, and *Bookslut*. He publishes and edits the online journal *Unpleasant Event Schedule*, and is an Assistant Professor of English at The College of Saint Rose in Albany, NY.

BRIAN O'CONNELL

THE SIX-FIGURE FREELANCER: TURNING YOUR PASSION FOR WRITING INTO PROFIT AND CAREER FULFILLMENT

Brian O'Connell
The Six-Figure Freelancer: Turning Your Passion For Writing
Into Profit And Career Fulfillment

WORKSHOP DESCRIPTION

Studies show that if Americans could do one thing over again, it would be to follow their passion into a career full of fun, fulfillment and profit. For writers of any age, it's certainly not too late to do that. In this workshop, you'll learn the secrets of a successful freelance writing career, It will walk you through each step necessary to plan, launch, sustain and profit from your own freelance-writing practice. Want to turn that burning desire inside of you to write and be published into reality—and change your career and your life in the process? That's what six-figure freelancing is all about.

INSTRUCTOR BIOGRAPHY

Brian O'Connell is a Bucks County, PA based freelance writer. A former Wall Street bond trader, O'Connell is the author of 15 books, including two bestsellers. His work has also appeared in publications like *The Wall Street Journal, Men's Health, USA Today, Cigar Magazine, CBS News Marketwatch, Newsweek*, and many others.

RACHEL PASTAN

WRITING OTHER PEOPLE'S SENTENCES

SUPPLEMENTARY MATERIALS:

SHORT STORY: *IN LOVE*

Rachel Pastan
Writing Other People's Sentences

WORKSHOP DESCRIPTION

Perhaps the most distinctive signature of any writer is the rhythm of his or her sentences: clean or baroque, lyrical or syncopated. Sometimes, however, we get locked into styles and forget that it's possible to write many kinds of sentences to create a whole range of effects. In this class we'll take paragraphs by writers with interesting prose styles—Munro, Drabble, Irving, and Roth—and rewrite the content while keeping the style intact, feeling what it's like to write prose we wouldn't have written ourselves

INSTRUCTOR BIOGRAPHY

Rachel Pastan teaches fiction writing at Swarthmore College, Her novel, *This Side of Married*, was published by Viking Press in 2004 and her second novel is forthcoming from Harcourt. A graduate of the University of Iowa Writers' Workshop and Harvard College, she has published short fiction in numerous magazines including *The Georgia Review, The Threepenny Review, and Mademoiselle.*

IN LOVE

after "Chemistry" by Carol Shields
For P. and S.

If you were to call me out of the blue, from New York, L.A., wherever, and remind me of those late nights we used to while away together in the Cafe Pamplona on the east end of the Square, and that you were the red-haired one, given to sarcasm and oversized sweaters and whose Norton Anthology of English Literature was cluttered and ripped with ballpoint scribbles, then I would, feigning a simple pleasure, try to smooth out my fraught remembrance of the winter of 1983. Or was it spring? I'm startled that I've forgotten, but one remembers the essentials; or perhaps not. One remembers what one remembers.

But you will remind me of the coffee, the limited menu—two kinds of sandwich, or a flan. The low ceiling, the tall waiters moving restlessly back and forth with their ridiculous trays. The spindly chairs in which we sat around the dime-sized tables, the three of us, huddled together, washed up on this ambiguous shore from the dark sea of Cambridge, wary with each other and mostly kind, each needing something which, ashamed and inarticulate despite our English majors, we are careful not to name.

You and he are in love—or so you sometimes say. Other times you insist it is only he who loves you, you have set your sights higher than his fish-white skin, his New Jersey upbringing, his devotion to the poet James Merrill. You don't speak his name. If we meet by chance in daylight in the middle of the frozen yard, you say, "Do you know what he did?" We are too intimate for names, those public roads by which strangers reach us, impersonal as telephone numbers, and as easily changed. You are each "he" to the other, and to me. I am the outsider, deferred to, politely included. Needed even, not so much as a mediator, but as a witness.

I have three suitemates. In our living room, the wind rattles the windows which overlook the street and the front of the Elks Club, where big-bellied men squeeze cans of beer on the concrete steps, and watch us come and go. We sit on the couch that once belonged to someone's brother, and play loud music, and sometimes laugh together over silly things. After a while, one girl returns to her desk, wearing her down jacket because the window doesn't entirely close; another goes off with a French boy, studying in the art library; the third takes her drawing pad and puts the headphones on, endlessly considerate. And I pretend to read poetry, and wait till nearly eleven, when I can throw my coat on and run across the windy street, to both of you.

He is already there, his wool scarf still wrapped around his neck, his black loafers shining. He smiles when I come in and half gets up. We do not touch. A waiter ambles by and I order coffee while unbuttoning my coat, and he begins to tell me how he called you last night at two AM and you were not there, and again at three, at four, at dawn.

I say, "Maybe the phone was unplugged."

He laughs unhappily.

"Anyway," I say. "I thought you left together. I thought you were going back to his place."

He stares gloomily into his coffee. "We had a fight. He began it."

"What about?" I have to ask; it's not something I relish.

He shrugs and glances back and forth, looking for the waiter, though his cup is nearly full. And I know we are verging on the territory where I cannot tread, that I cannot even begin to imagine—and which, truthfully, I do not want to imagine. The midnight, treacherous earth of your love.

Now you arrive, only a sweater despite the wintry night, despite the long walk down Garden Street. When you lean over and kiss my cheek, you infuse me with your chill. "You're warm," you say, and pull a chair close beside me, tapping the waiter and ordering hot chocolate and a noche sandwich before you turn your head far enough to see him. "Oh hello," you say, then turn back to me. "Did he tell you what he did?"

Your voice is beautiful. Sharp as a good kitchen knife, but nicely modulated, a roaring hum in it like a distant lawn mower.

I shake my head. "What?"

"He hit me."

This is plainly not believable, and I say so. My opinion carries weight—which may be why I am here. I look from one of you to the other. In spite of your anger, his shame, you both look secretly pleased.

"He hit me," you repeat, and take my hand. You look at him across the table, and he looks back. The energy of your gaze sparks the air blue.

The truth, these many years later, is indeterminate. It hovers above me, beyond me, out of reach. The truth is, I don't remember which one of you it was who did the hitting, which thin cheek was reddened (for in my mind the hit was a slap, no punchers you). Already I think of you as almost one—a pair, a matched set, down to the same shoe size.

And I, in my wide hips, hiding behind my hair—who was I to you? Did you know the way my heart tripped when you smiled your sly smile? Did you count on it? Wasn't I any of a dozen smart girls you might have chosen, a dozen daisies? Sweet flowers, but cheaply picked.

If we run into one another on the street tomorrow, you will not recognize me. I have cut my hair, and I know how to choose my clothes; I know how to choose.

Oh, this is anger speaking, anger's oily residue! How will I know whether you recognize me? And how will I recognize you? Two men, where boys were. As married as I am. Yet sometimes at night I dream about you. I dream you waiting for me in the cafe, your coffee cooling in your wide cups, your arms outstretched. Every day of my life I am poised to rush into them, to be again a part of what we were. We have never said goodbye to each other—that is a small, good thing. Like not using names, it is an intimacy. A kind of pact, as, when a storm or some other accident severs a telephone conversation, it is understood that someone will call the other back. It is just a matter of time, a matter of waiting for the storm to clear.

Some storms, like some loves, are longer than others.

SUSAN PERLOFF

WRITER'S BLOCK AND CREATIVITY

SUPPLEMENTARY MATERIALS:

HANDOUT: OVERCOMING WRITER'S BLOCK

ARTICLE: *WHY CAN'T JOHNNY WRITE?*

Susan Perloff
Writer's Block and Creativity

WORKSHOP DESCRIPTION

If it's difficult to draft the first sentence or paragraph—or if you stall suddenly along the way—this session is for you. Learn easy but powerful ways to break through your own resistance. Once you recognize the nuanced stages of writing and your individual writing process, you're on the way to exploring your own creativity, within this session and beyond. Any level.

INSTRUCTOR BIOGRAPHY

Susan Perloff is a freelance writer, editor and writing coach. She writes for corporate and institutional clients in print and electronic media and is the author of *Pennsylvania Off the Beaten Path*. She has been teaching adults to write for nearly 20 years. Her byline has appeared more than 120 times in *The Philadelphia Inquirer* and in more than 100 other periodicals.

Overcoming Writer's Block

If you give in to writer's block, how can you pay the mortgage?
If you encounter a bad case of writer's block, try these suggestions.

1. Draft a sentence describing your writing project. Let it flow from that.

2. Type: "Dear Mother, I am having an awful time trying to begin a piece of writing. It just won't work. You see, I am supposed to write a report for my boss about . . . ." Keep on writing about what you don't want to write about.

3. Start anywhere you want to start. Jump in wherever you wish: at the end, with an anecdote, or with the three "bullets" that will appear on page five. No English teacher is peering over your shoulder, critiquing your system.

4. Change your approach. If you normally outline but you can't get started, skip the outline. If you never outline but you can't get started, try outlining. Type if you normally write long-hand. Write long-hand if you normally type. Splurge on a fountain pen and purple ink.

5. Write about anything for 10 minutes, ignoring punctuation, spelling and grammar. Writing about *something* may lead you to write about your desired topic. Write about RAIN or IF I HAD or YESTERDAY. If this trick works for you, fill a file with potential topics, picking blindly when you need inspiration. (For more, read Natalie Goldberg's *Writing Down the Bones.*)

6. When you feel stuck, switch gears. Clean your files. Attack another writing project. Pull weeds. Allow your unconscious mind time to solve the problem.

7. Discuss your intended topic with co-workers, who are familiar with the issue. They may help you determine a better way to go.

8. Discuss your topic with people at home, who aren't familiar. Explaining the material to them may help you clarify your thoughts.

9. Specify an amount of time to write. When time is up, stop—and start fresh tomorrow. If you don't have that luxury, designate the time you will write this morning and return this afternoon.

10. Try the salami technique. Cut large projects into smaller bite-size accomplishable slices. Write one at a time. (This works for hiking, too: "Climb to the next tree, and we'll sit on that rock.")

11. Know your clear-thinking and muddled times of the day. Plan to write when you can think clearly.

12. Imitate Helen Gurley Brown, founder and editor of *Cosmopolitan*. When she had trouble thinking of cover-lines, or shout-outs, for *Cosmo*, she captured her husband, David, and rode around Central Park, not letting him out until he came up with good lines.

13. Listen to Vincent Van Gogh, who said, "If you hear a voice within you saying, 'You are not a painter,' then by all means paint, and that voice will be silenced." For you, just write, and you will know you are a writer.

14. Don't be discouraged. Every writer has trouble writing."

15. Reward yourself.

16. Get naked, as Victor Hugo is rumored to have done. The author of *The Hunchback of Notre Dame* and *Les Misérables* removed his clothes, gave them to his servant and asked for the clothes to be returned in several hours.

Why Can't Johnny Write?
by Susan Perloff
June 9, 2004, in *Metro Philly*

Why can't Johnny write? Because his teachers can't.

In Philadelphia 43 percent of high-school English teachers flunked the recent Pennsylvania State System of Assessment exam in English, a basic test to determine if they are fit to teach. Send your kid to school to study rocket science—and the instructor can't even pass Astronomy 101.

Johnny can't write, and neither can his daddy nor his teacher nor his godmother nor his older brother. For 15 years I have taught writing to 300-plus adults, most of whom have college degrees. Dermatologists, bankruptcy lawyers and corporate public relations executives cannot manage subject-verb agreement. Engineers don't know what's wrong with "between you and I." Since risk analysts don't know if they want fame or notoriety, they should've went to better schools.

But what schools could they have attended? Adults claim that everything they ever needed to know about grammar they learned from Sister Maria in third grade or Mrs. Benson in 11th. They sit open-mouthed when they hear that everything they ever learned about quotation marks is wrong. Some memorized the "rule" that one should delete all commas in sentences unless there's a pause, while others cling to the "truism" that you can, never, have, too, many commas.

Five years ago a man hired me to teach his corporate-advertising staff to switch to active verbs, find telling metaphors and write parallel lists. Went great. Weeks later he introduced me to his wife, an English teacher in a Philadelphia high school. Proudly she told me that her students don't like grammar, so she doesn't teach it.

Like, uh, thank you for increasing the future stream of adults needing a writing coach?

Recently Roger Shattuck, university professor emeritus at Boston University, helped screen the five finalists for the English-teacher vacancy at Mount Abraham Union High School in Bristol, Vermont, where he served on the school board. He invited the candidates to say what they could about *Gulliver's Travels*. "Some got nowhere," he says.

He asked what comments they would make if these sentences showed up in students' writing.

1. Laying on the surface of the water, I was sure the fish must be dead. (This sentence contains two errors. First is a dangling modifier: "I" am on the water, not the fish. And "laying" should be "lying.")
2. When you leave, please bring your notebook with you. ("Take me out to the ballgame," Shattuck corrects. "*Take* something to another place. *Bring* something back from there.")
3. We still remember the trick you played on my sister and me. ("The sentence is correct, but every applicant tried to fix it.")

Not one of five people got the three sentences right, but one of the five people got the gig and is presumably teaching high-school English today.

Shattuck says, "So many teachers come through educational curricula. They can take a class called 'English for teachers' and be done with it."

Teachers have a tough job. Many kids don't go to school able or eager to learn. Reading for pleasure has given way to watching television and playing computer games. Yesteryear, dummies dropped out of school in eighth grade, while today they receive diplomas and dorm space. Fewer kids speak the same language, literally, and teachers may have scant minutes allotted to teaching writing.

I have no grievance against the teaching profession, since adults in all métiers continue to produce volumes of woeful writing. People consider themselves good writers, which, one determines after reading a paragraph of their "verbage" (sic), means that they feel comfortable writing, not that they write well.

Somebody has to write newspapers, proposals and petitions, but adult Julies by the jillions cannot write a cogent paragraph. They don't care. They think it doesn't matter if they use good words in proper sequence. Use quotations to spice up the report? Recognize a verbal? Today someone said the word *gerund* is jargon.

OK, Julie. Listen up, Johnny. Let's start fresh. Sit in a quiet place. Now, please, write about what you like and don't like about writing. How long? Until you're done. Tomorrow we'll read it together. Write like Nike runs: Just do it.

DAVID PRETE

THE ART OF PUBLIC READINGS

David Prete
The Art of Public Readings

WORKSHOP DESCRIPTION

Giving public readings is a crucial part of being a writer of any genre—a chance to show your audience how good your writing is and gives your work the readership it deserves. However, most readings suffer because authors can't take the power of their words off the page in public. This workshop, led by actor, author and professional readings coach David Prete (who studied acting under Academy Award winning director Mike Nichols and is a W.W. Norton published author) will teach writers to develop techniques essential for good readings: relaxation, vocal variation, rhythm, emotional expression, and connecting to audiences so listeners feel they're being told a story one on one. This course will help with public speaking of all kinds. Participants will bring a work in progress or completed piece, which will be read aloud to the class, and the instructor will work with them individually to develop these readings.

INSTRUCTOR BIOGRAPHY

David Prete is a writer, actor and readings coach living in New York City. He graduated from the New Actors Workshop where he studied with Mike Nichols, Tony and Academy Award winning director of *The Graduate, Primary Colors, The Birdcage, Angels in America,* and George Morrison, who also taught Dustin Hoffman, Edie Falco, Gene Hackman, and others. He was last seen in the new Off Broadway play *On the Line* at New York's historic Cherry Lane Theater. He co-founded Water Theatre Company where he worked as an actor and producer. He has also been seen in independent films screened at the Santa Barbara Film Festival, the Long Island Film Festival, and the International Film Festival of NYC. He teaches writers to read their work in front of audiences at conferences and schools around the country, including a graduate course at The New School in New York City called "The Art of Public Readings." W.W. Norton published his first book, *Say That to My Face*, in 2003. He is currently at work on a novel entitled, *Bones of His Bones*, also to be published by Norton. For More information visit: *www.davidprete.com.*

FRANK QUATTRONE

BREAKING OUT TO BREAK IN

Frank Quattrone
Breaking Out To Break In

WORKSHOP DESCRIPTION

There are more closet writers out there than you could possibly imagine. However, many are unpublished because they don[1]t know how to get themselves, and their work, noticed, or have no idea how to transform personal experience (such as travel, attendance at cultural events and so forth) into something worthy of publication. This workshop will explore several ways fledgling writers can break out of their shells and into print in newspapers and magazines. Some enticing in-class exercises will encourage participants to escape their self-imposed shackles.

INSTRUCTOR BIOGRAPHY

Frank D. Quattrone, managing editor and principal writer for *Ticket,* Montgomery Newspapers[1] award-winning weekly guide to entertainment and the arts, is also a regular contributor to *Montgomery County Town & Country Living, Chester County Town & Country Living,* and *Bucks County Town & Country Living.* After a 24-year career as an English professor, College for 24 years, he now teaches journalism at Penn State Abington College and is faculty advisor to *The Lion's Roar,* the campus newspaper. Since 2002, he has taught copyediting, magazine and features publication, book marketing and more in Rosemont College's graduate program in English & Publishing. Author of Arcadia Publishing Company's *Ambler* volume in its *Images of America* series, he is also a board member of the Philadelphia Writers' Conference.

BARRY RAINE

LITERARY NON-FICTION MASTER CLASS

Barry Raine
Literary Non-Fiction Master Class

WORKSHOP DESCRIPTION

The term "creative writing" is often used to describe works of fiction, whether they are short stories or novels. But too often, some of the best "creative" writing is overlooked because it is non-fiction that is written in a literary, novelistic way while using real-life characters and events to build a strong narrative line. This 4-hour intensive Literary Non-Fiction Master Class will explore the craft of writing compelling non-fiction through hands-on instruction and by using examples from books as well as magazines such as *The New Yorker, The Atlantic Monthly, Harper's and Brick*, among many others. The work of such highly regarded contemporary non-fiction writers as Lawrence Wright, Susan Orlean, Jane Kramer and William Langewiesche and other emerging literary non-fiction luminaries will be analyzed and discussed to teach students about structure, tone, chronology and how to incorporate the many other elements a writer needs to write arresting non-fiction articles and books. By focusing on the best non-fiction, students will come away with a far better understanding of the stylistic devices, keen observation and overall selectivity that leads to excellence in all writing.

(Note: This class does not address the techniques of business writing. The focus is solely on literary journalism.)

INSTRUCTOR BIOGRAPHY

Barry Raine is an editor, writer and journalist who has written for *Men's Journal, Salon.com, Newsweek International* and *The Ontario Review*, among other publications. His first book, *Where the River Bends*, was published in May 2002. His second book, *Grounds for*

Sculpture: Iconography and the Three-Dimensional Image will be published in December 2006. A native of New Orleans, he now lives and works in New York City.

KATHRYN RHETT

THE NONFICTION NARRATOR

Kathryn Rhett
The Nonfiction Narrator

WORKSHOP DESCRIPTION

This workshop invites writers to consider the deliberate creation of the nonfiction narrator, the character development of that narrator, and the role the narrator plays in literary nonfiction. We will discuss point of view, tone, and the distance between narrator and subject with reference to various models of lyric, journalistic and narrative nonfiction. How does the nonfiction narrator effectively engage the reader, express the subject, and serve as a unifying element for a piece of writing? We will discuss strategies for creating and refining a nonfiction narrator who is not only accurate and truthful, but who also best serves the work at hand.

INSTRUCTOR BIOGRAPHY

Kathryn Rhett is an associate professor of English at Gettysburg College, and is the author of *Near Breathing*, a memoir, and editor of the anthology *Survival Stories: Memoirs of Crisis*. She publishes nonfiction and poetry in literary journals such as *Crab Orchard Review, Creative Nonfiction, Harvard Review, Michigan Quarterly Review*, and *Ploughshares*, as well as personal essays in massmarket magazines such as *Real Simple*, and reviews in *The Chicago Tribune* and *Ploughshares*. She has taught at Johns Hopkins University, the University of Iowa, University of San Francisco, and University of North Carolina at Charlotte, as well as in summer workshops at the Iowa Summer Writing Festival and the Fine Arts Work Center at Provincetown. Currently, in addition to teaching memoir and essay writing at Gettysburg, she is a core faculty member of the low-residency M.F.A. program at Queens University in Charlotte.

MARY LOU ROBERTS

CREATIVE FREELANCING IN THE CORPORATE WORLD

Mary Lou Roberts
Creative Freelancing in the Corporate World

WORKSHOP DESCRIPTION

While you're waiting for the payoff on your Great American Novel, you have bills to pay. At the same time, corporations are often desperately looking for people who can write. If you know how to connect with these companies, you can turn a freelance writing business into a profitable enterprise. This session will give you tips on how to build a resume and portfolio that will attract their attention, connect with the right companies and people, price your services, and deliver a quality product that will keep them coming back for more. It will also dispel the myth that business writing is not creative. Indeed, good business writing, while not fictional, is good problem-solving that taps into the hearts and minds of your audience.

INSTRUCTOR BIOGRAPHY

Mary Lou Roberts earned a B.A. in English from DePaul University and an M.A. in Humanities from Arcadia University. In her 37-year career she has specialized in business writing and communications with a focus on technology for companies such as Time, Inc., Blue Cross and Blue Shield, Honeywell Information Systems, and Computer Sciences Corporation. In her own consulting business, she has for many high-tech companies and has published more than 500 news and feature articles as a contributor to print and online journals such as *Computerworld, Information Week*, and *IT Jungle*. She also teaches composition, business writing, and communications courses at Arcadia and Bucks County Community College. She has written two unpublished children's books and is currently working on a mystery series based on her Newfoundland dogs.

LARI ROBLING

THE CRAFT OF FOOD WRITING

Lari Robling
The Craft of Food Writing

WORKSHOP DESCRIPTION

Bring your writing skills to the table. You enjoy writing and eating . . . learn how to combine the two! Discover the many aspects of food writing: writing a recipe in proper format; creating recipe headers that make you hungry; identifying recipes with photographic interest; and using food as a hook to tell a larger story. We'll get an overview of the many kinds of food writing from restaurant reviews to cookbooks, magazine articles and broadcast. Learn how to slant your pitch, when an agent is necessary, and what are some common pitfalls.

INSTRUCTOR BIOGRAPHY

Lari Robling is the author of *Endangered Recipes: Too Good to be Forgotten*, published by Stewart, Tabori & Chang. She's also the associate producer of "A Chef's Table," a nationally syndicated public radio show produced by WHYY. Robling has worked in test kitchens for major corporations and magazines and has styled food for publications as well as written numerous articles. She loves Philadelphia restaurants—especially the neighborhood BYO—but most enjoys cooking at home with friends.

MAYA ROCK

THE ART OF THE QUERY LETTER

Maya Rock
The Art of the Query Letter

WORKSHOP DESCRIPTION

Maya Rock, a junior agent at Writers House, will explain why the query letter is such a vital and important part to getting your book published and show participants how to create the best letter for their work. She'll also to discuss how to submit to agents and how to deal with rejections as well as offers of representation. Class will include sample query letters plus a "tip sheet."

INSTRUCTOR BIOGRAPHY

Maya Rock is a junior agent at Writers House. After graduating from Princeton in 2002, she worked as an assistant at Anderson Grinberg Literary Management where she quickly realized agenting was what she wanted to do. Her most recent sale was a memoir to Regan Books, *Gone To The Crazies* by Alison Weaver.

CARLIN ROMANO

CULTURAL CRITICISM

Carlin Romano
Cultural Criticism

WORKSHOP DESCRIPTION

"Everyone's a critic!" some newspapers and magazine declare these days. Blogging and interactive kibbitzing of all kinds, we're told, are taking over the universe. So what's to learn about criticism? It's as easy as talking. You open your mouth and if what comes out isn't entirely positive, you're a critic. (Well, you might be a dribbler, but that's another story.) This class is for those, from beginners to established critics, who believe there's more to it than that. We'll discuss what distinguishes superb and mediocre criticism. We'll discuss point of view, reportorial obligations, whether the critic should entertain, whether the critic should defer to artists under consideration, how criticism does or doesn't differ from reviewing. Feel invited to bring copies of a review you've written that's 700 words or shorter. There's no guarantee we'll talk about yours—but we might.

INSTRUCTOR BIOGRAPHY

Carlin Romano is literary critic of *The Philadelphia Inquirer*, Critic-at-Large of the *Chronicle of Higher Education* and a former President of the National Book Critics Circle, the nationwide organization of more than 600 literary critics, editors and scholars. Before joining *The Inquirer*, Romano worked at *The Washington Post* and *The New York Daily News*. He also served as Critic-at-Large of *Lingua Franca* and literary columnist at *The Village Voice*. Over the years, his criticism has appeared in *The Nation, The New Yorker, Harper's, Slate, Salon, Tikkun, The Weekly Standard* and other national publications. He is a 3-time winner of the Society of Professional Journalists First Prize in Criticism, and a recipient of the Commonwealth of Pennsylvania's Distinguished Arts Criticism Award. In 2005, he was one of three finalists, along with

Frank Rich of The New York Times and Joseph Morgenstern of *The Wall Street Journal*, for the Pulitzer Prize in Criticism. (Morgenstern won.) The Pulitzer Board cited Romano "for bringing new vitality to the classic essay across a formidable array of topics."

LYNN ROSEN

HOW TO WRITE A BOOK PROPOSAL

SUPPLEMENTARY MATERIALS:

HANDOUT: A LETTER TO AN AUTHOR FROM AN AGENT

Lynn Rosen
How to Write a Book Proposal

WORKSHOP DESCRIPTION

The book proposal is the document used by authors (and their literary representatives) to pitch books to publishers. It is the author's chance to show off his or her writing skills and credentials, to give a sense of the scope and content of the book, and to convince the publisher of the need for the proposed book in the marketplace. Given its importance, every element of a book proposal must be carefully composed. This workshop will teach the participant the elements of a good book proposal and help them answer the questions a proposal should address, such as: What is the book about? Why am I the one to write it? Who will buy this book and why? What other books exist in the category? The workshop will also address how to develop and evaluate a book concept. It will include an overview of the trade book publishing chain from author to bookseller, as well as a review of important publishing job descriptions, including author, literary agent, book packager, publisher, editor, and retailer. This course is appropriate for all levels.

INSTRUCTOR BIOGRAPHY

Lynn Rosen has had a wide-ranging twenty-plus year career in book publishing as an editor, literary agent, book packager, and author. As an editor, Lynn worked with publishers of adult trade non-fiction and illustrated gift books. She served as Editorial Director at Peter Pauper Press, an independent publisher of gift books, and as Senior Editor at Running Press. Earlier in her career, Lynn was an Editor in the Trade Division of Ballantine Books, a division of Random House. In 1991, Lynn launched Leap First, an independent literary agency and book packager, which she ran until 1999. Lynn has also worked in retail as a bookseller and Community Relations Manager at Barnes & Noble. Lynn is the author of two new books, The Baby Owner's Games and Activities Book (Quirk Books, Fall 2006) and Elements of the Table: A Simple Guide for Hosts and Guests (Clarkson Potter, Spring 2007). (Find out more about Lynn's books at www.lynnrosen.com) Lynn graduated from the University of Pennsylvania with an Honors degree in English, and holds a Masters in English and Comparative Literature from Columbia University. She lives in the Philadelphia area.

A Letter to an Author from an Agent
by Lynn Rosen

Dear Writer,

I know you're feeling really optimistic about your work and excited about the possibility of becoming a published author. I'm excited for you. The passion you bring to your work makes it a real pleasure to work with you and others like you.

I hate to sound a negative note, but I feel I must be realistic and warn you that the path to publication is, as they say, a bumpy ride. You are about to face a big challenge, and a lot of rejection. Is your skin toughened? Are you ready to persevere, and not to take rejection personally? OK, then, let's begin.

I ran my own literary agency for eight years. Over that time, I received hundreds (maybe thousands) of queries from writers like you, people who want to get a book published, be it a first book or just a new book. You've been instructed that you need an agent to help you. And while once I would have told you that an enterprising author could go it alone, now I would say that obtaining the representation of an agent is the wisest course. A good agent will make the process easier, and most publishers prefer to work with agents.

Step 1: Educate Yourself

Before you even begin to contact agents, you should know something about the process of getting published. The more informed you are, the better you will be able to negotiate this course, and the better an impression you will make.

There's nothing I appreciated more than an intelligent query letter and a knowledgeable potential client. There are many good books available about getting published. Familiarize yourself with some of these books and learn the steps a book takes from manuscript to publication. You'll find these books at a library or at the bookstore in the reference/writing section.

Step 2: Prepare a Proposal

This step takes a lot of time and work. What you submit to an agent has to be good. Once I received a query letter that said: "I know my book needs more editing, but I wanted to show it to you and see what you thought." Not! If you know your book needs more work, do the work before you take up an agent's time. Send it out when you think it's perfect. Which is not to say you won't then receive editorial critiques, but at least the agent will be reading a polished work.

If you are submitting fiction, your proposal is your manuscript, or several sample chapters, along with a good cover letter and perhaps a synopsis. If you are submitting nonfiction, your proposal includes an overview; a section on marketing and competition; a section on you, the author; a brief chapter-by-chapter outline; and some sample chapters. Again, consult some of the many good books on proposal writing.

Step 3: Compile a List of Agents

How do you classify what you are writing? Is it genre fiction: romance, mystery, science fiction? Is it narrative journalism? Self-help? Try and fit your work into a general category for the purpose of identifying the appropriate agents to approach.

Start by taking a careful look through several of the books that list agents. In most of these books, the listings include a description of the type of book agents are seeking. Pay attention to this, and only send them what they say they want. I rejected 50 percent of the proposals I received because they were for types of books I didn't represent. You could be the next Julia Child, but I'd probably have rejected you because I didn't represent cookbooks.

Add to your list of possible agents by networking. Ask for referrals from other writers you know, or find names from other sources like writers' conferences and Web sites. Another great technique—look at published books that are in your category and that you admire. Check the acknowledgments page and see who the agent is—they're usually thanked! When you write to them, be sure to mention the book in which you found their name and why you admire it.

Step 4: Send out your submission

You've got your proposal ready, along with your list of agents. Time to get it in the mail!

Most agents prefer mail queries, whether e-mail or USPS. Most also strongly dislike telephone queries. (My least favorite were authors who deliberately called after hours, so that I would have to call them back on my dime. I didn't!) I liked to sit down on my own schedule with a pile of queries, and a letter gave me an immediate sense of how a potential client wrote.

There's some question about whether a query letter should go alone or with a proposal/writing sample. If you're using snail mail, a letter alone is quicker and saves postage. That way, if the agent isn't interested, he or she can tell you immediately not to bother shipping a whole lot of paper. And if they want to see more, they'll let you know.

If you're sending an electronic query, I suggest just a letter, because people don't like getting attachments from unknown addresses. Again, let the agent read your letter, and they'll request a proposal if they want more. Then you can ask them about how to send it.

Always write an intelligent, realistic cover letter. Tell concisely what you are writing and what your qualifications are in relation to your topic. Don't tell an agent you're sending "a guaranteed bestseller" (spare them!), or that all your family and friends think you're a great writer (of course they do!). Just be straightforward, and tell the agent what you think is distinct about the book.

And always, always, make sure you make it easy for the agent to respond, either by including your e-mail address or enclosing a SASE (self-addressed stamped envelope). If agents are giving you their time and trained editorial judgment for free, the least you can do is pay the postage!

A note on simultaneous submissions: I didn't object to this—I think it's more realistic. Just be sure to tell the agents that you are doing this. Say something in your query letter like: "Several other agents are also considering this proposal."

Step 5: Follow Up

After a period of time has passed after submission (1 month to 6 weeks), I think a follow-up phone call is appropriate. Keep it brief and polite. Call to say you're following up to find out the status of your submission. A polite call from an author often caused me to elevate a proposal to the top of the stack (and do keep in mind how tall this stack was!).

Step 6: Persevere

Unless you're very lucky, it's going to take a while. You'll get a bunch of rejections and maybe some agents won't respond at all. Many who are considering your submission may take longer to do so than you would like. But if you believe in yourself and your work, and persevere, you will ultimately prevail.

Once you've succeeded in finding an agent, the process will begin all over again when your agent makes submissions to publishers. However, you'll then have your agent as your advocate, to guide you successfully through to publication.

Good luck!

Sincerely,
Lynn Rosen

This article was originally published at *www.writedirections.com*

MICHELE ROSEN

INTRODUCTION TO WEBLOGS

Michele Rosen
Introduction to Weblogs

WORKSHOP DESCRIPTION

Weblogs are the fastest growing form of publishing today, with more than 75,000 new weblogs created every day. If you want to join the blogosphere or just learn what it's all about, then this course is for you. Whether you write fiction, nonfiction, or poetry, weblogs can be a wonderful avenue for practicing your writing and developing an audience. A few weblogs have even resulted in offers for book deals! During the course, we'll cover the short but exciting history of weblogs, take a look at examples of some of the best weblogs, explore the wide variety of topics and writing styles that can result in a great weblog, and even learn how to create a weblog yourself! No technical experience is required, although some comfort with surfing the Internet is recommended.

INSTRUCTOR BIOGRAPHY

Michele Rosen is an instructor in the journalism department at Rowan University, where she teaches courses in website production, online writing, and desktop publishing. Some of her students' work can be seen at *http://www.rowanbuzz.com*. She has worked as a writer, editor, and producer for a number of websites, including *forbes.com*, *space.com*, and *zdnet.com*. She was co-founder and vice president of content strategy for *iAnalyst.com*, a financial services website. You can visit her blog at *http://inserttechhere.blogspot.com*. Previously, Michele worked as a newspaper reporter for the Courier Post and as a magazine editor for technology industry trade magazines. Her freelance work has been published in *The New York Times* and *Wired* magazine. Michele has a master's degree in journalism from New York University is currently pursuing an MFA in creative writing at Rosemont College.

SABRINA RUBIN ERDELY

THE ART OF DESCRIPTION AND THE "TELLING" DETAIL

Sabrina Rubin Erdely
The Art of Description and the "Telling" Detail

WORKSHOP DESCRIPTION

When you're creating the kind of non-fiction writing that makes readers feel like they're really "there," the details make all the difference. But too often, writers swamp their prose with details that simply make their writing bloated or, even worse, generic. So how much detail should you reveal, and what kind? We'll discuss the art of the "telling detail," the type that makes your writing feel specific, immediate and true. In addition, we'll talk about how to apply those well-chosen details to virtually every aspect of writing—from character description to dialogue to scene setting—and bring your writing to life. To that end, please bring a short (under 500 words) sample of your own non-fiction work—one you feel comfortable reading aloud—for class discussion.

INSTRUCTOR BIOGRAPHY

Sabrina Rubin Erdely is an award-winning feature writer and investigative journalist. She is a Writer-at-Large at *Philadelphia Magazine*, a Contributing Writer at *SELF*, and a freelancer for national magazines; her work has appeared in *GQ, The New Yorker, Mother Jones* and *LIFE*, among other publications, and has been anthologized in *Best American Crime Writing*. Erdely's writing and reporting have earned her a number of prestigious awards, including a National Magazine Award nomination.

LISA RUDY

WRITING AND THE WEB:
USING THE INTERNET TO CREATE AND
SELL YOUR WRITING

Lisa Rudy
**Writing And The Web: Using The Internet To Create And
Sell Your Writing**

WORKSHOP DESCRIPTION

Discover the Web as a writer's best friend. Learn techniques for finding
the information you need, whether you're looking for historic factoids
or publishers' idelines. Dive into the world of blogging, and learn
about E-zines and other Web-based writing opportunities. Consider
creating your own writer's website. Please note: this is NOT a technical
workshop, and does not include information about how to design or
post your own website.

INSTRUCTOR BIOGRAPHY

Since starting her freelance business in 1991, **Lisa Jo Rudy** has
worked with clients ranging from museums and universities to
federal agencies and multinational corporations. Her credits include
numerous books, print and online publications, and a wide variety
of educational and multimedia projects. Lisa is also the *About.com*
Guide to Autism Spectrum Disorders (*About.com* is a New York Times
Company website).

SAVANNAH SCHROLL-GUZ

THE COSMOS OF INDIE LIT:
A CONSTELLATION OF PRESSES AND 'ZINES:

SUPPLEMENTARY MATERIALS:

EXCERPT: *CONSUMED: WOMEN ON EXCESS*
"American Soma"

Savannah Schroll-Guz
The Cosmos of Indie Lit:
A Constellation of Presses and 'Zines:

WORKSHOP DESCRIPTION

Indie literature no longer means photocopied broadsheets sold at launch parties. It now means trade paperbacks with wide distribution and acknowledgement by mainstream media. Works published by indie presses frequently have instant cachet and offer the potential for cult following. In some cases, they are even the stepping stones to broader, more traditional markets. Indie presses are often very accessible to new writers and allow authors a great deal of control over final products. From the infamous Soft Skull and Graywolf presses to up-and-coming publishing entities like Better Non Sequitur, this workshop will explore the varied and hierarchical world of indie lit, with a brief survey of the monthly and quarterly web-based indie 'zines that welcome work from new writers and often pave the way to book-length publications. Students will receive a list of press and editorial contact information as well as tips for making successful queries from an instructor who is currently part of the indie publishing circle.

INSTRUCTOR BIOGRAPHY

Savannah Schroll-Guz is a member of So New Media's editorial board, quarterly guest editor for the web version of the indie literary journal, *Hobart* (*www.hobartpulp.com*), and creative nonfiction editor for *Subterranean Quarterly*. She is author of the short story collection *The Famous & The Anonymous* (San Diego: Better Non Sequitur, 2004) and editor of the anthology, *Consumed: Women on Excess* (Frankfurt: So New Media, 2005). She has also been a guest castaway on *Desert Island Discs* with Ellen Hughes. Her essays and reviews have appeared in *The European Journal of Cultural Studies*, Johns Hopkins'

Modernism/Modernity, and *Creative Nonfiction*, and she is a regular contributor to *Library Journal*. She lives with her husband in West Virginia's northern panhandle and is currently working on a second collection of short fiction.

Originally appearing in Consumed: Women on Excess *(Frankfurt: So New Media, 2005)*

American Soma
Savannah Schroll-Guz

We noticed it first—we, who I like to think of as the extremely sensitive people, the ones endowed with an unpleasant aptitude for sinking to the very floorboards of despair and feeling the pulses of ugly truth that surge underneath them. I carry splinters in both my palms, and I've sniffed the traces of hopelessness that leak like sewer gas through cracks in the parquet. My friend David called us highly intelligent. He said we should look at it as a gift, like ESP, but I've never felt that way. If I could live my life as a happy person and give up some of this awareness, I would.

That summer and fall, David and I became temporarily unable to plumb the depths of our depression. The far-reaching but invisible ramifications of misery were no longer registering on our sonar. And it seemed to take place overnight. In the months preceding the election that year, something happened to the entire nation. We were collectively overcome by a rash of good feeling.

Never before had I not been able to think a situation all the way through to its logical end. I often repeated my analyses over and over until I found myself mired yet again in desolation. At the time, I did not know any other way. My wiring ran on well-established pathways. Suddenly, however, in the heat of summer, there was a comforting insulation beneath me. It separated me from my habitual despondency. I sat in my apartment and felt content. To simply breathe was a pleasure. I looked up instead of down, and I began to notice the black squirrels in the building's courtyard, the pansies in the cement planter outside my office building. Food never tasted so good. Coffee was better each time I had it. I could not explain what was happening to me, although I dreamily considered that I might be outgrowing my defects.

David, too, lost his capacity for sensing the world's hidden horror. We met for coffee, both of us happier than we had been since childhood. The notion that we were one degree away from lives we both feared, that microbes would invade our bodies, that anger, loathing, and filth would prevail dissipated entirely. I looked at them as ridiculous fixations I could no longer understand. David was less sanguine about the change in his perceptive powers. He thought it was unusual that we should both experience the phenomenon at the same time. "It's gotta be something environmental. The fucking trees won't bud next year or the fish will start popping up dead in the Potomac. Then we'll know. Something's going on. Start watching the papers."

We actually hadn't noticed, but two years before, the FDA, in conjunction with the Department of Health and Human Services, had appointed a special committee to examine American eating habits. It was conducted during the height of the Atkins and South Beach trends, and in light of the countrywide preoccupation with weight, it did not seem particularly significant. Apparently, the most popular food in America was found to be pizza, despite all the low-carb proselytizing done by dieting gurus and marketing firms engaged by corporations looking for the next big cash-in. Soda, beer, and coffee were determined to be the most consumed beverages.

The government would not have needed to convene a special commission to gather this data. Committee officials would have been able to determine this at any staff meeting involving food or simply by watching what their aides and interns sat beside their keyboards each morning. But Washington runs on the dawdling conclusions drawn by administrative agencies. If things were done any more efficiently, much of the government might find itself redundant. And, true, the executive officials who actually ordered the inquiry live differently. They, who look down from their vaulted civil buildings onto cities awash in coffee and beer, themselves look forward to single malt scotch, rare sherry, and Amarone the color of bull's blood. Perhaps this is what prevented them from feeling so content over those few blissful months. Or maybe they all just knew what to avoid. *Coffee in the morning? Hell no. How about a Screwdriver or a Bloody Mary? Now there's the breakfast of champions.*

In retrospect, I suppose the real impetus for the investigation was to determine how to reach the most people. What medium was the most democratic, cutting across all ethnic and economic boundaries? How would both rural and urban populations be reached? Would children be harmed by high doses? Neurological experts were consulted on the effect of chemical catalysts on humans of various weights and age groups. It was collectively decided that broad-based clinical trials would be conducted first in metropolitan areas, where the effects would be closely monitored.

Starbucks was approached first. "You have the potential to make more money than you have ever seen before," were the first words from the official's mouth during his initial phone call. Several top drawer meetings ensued, during which CEOs and high-ranking government representatives, a decorated military general among them, discussed the possibilities. The last conference commenced at 1:00 p.m. on a balmy Seattle afternoon. It lasted exactly two hours. A rolling humidor holding the chairman's finest cigars, foreign contraband among them, was brought in at 1:45 p.m. A smaller cart, containing a variety of brandies, was wheeled in shortly thereafter. Hands shook at 2:45 and departure was taken by the federal representatives at 3 p.m. It was done.

Deals were subsequently tendered to the national pizza chains, the two major soft drink producers, the three most successful nationally-distributing breweries, and two of the largest coffee manufacturers, whose products were sold exclusively in grocery stores. Each company was lead to believe they would enjoy exclusivity and therefore, have a decisive edge over competitors. This made the proposal particularly compelling.

The circle of knowledge was kept small. Only one or two people within each organization were aware of what was newly introduced into company recipes. The bags, when they arrived, were without labels. They contained a non-descript yellowish-looking powder. The only lingering question was how the powder's chemical composition would respond when exposed to heat. Consequently, testing was done using pharmaceutical-grade microspheres, and the results were successful. Without further delay, the microspheric powder was mixed with the dry ingredients of crust dough and stirred into beverage syrups with the customary thoughtlessness of unsuspecting employees. Initially, it was found that its inclusion in brewer's yeast inhibited the fermentation process of beer. So the powder was liquefied and poured into production tanks before bottling.

Before being ground, whole coffee beans were soaked in a marinade of the special powder dissolved in water. It was treated by corporate HQ as the company's secret ingredient and was measured out and added to frappuccinos, ciders, and chais. It made its clandestine appearance in every beverage on the menu. Skim mocha? Espresso doppio? A double whip-whip latte? Without fail. It could not be escaped.

We could not see it, but the vesicles of our cerebral cortexes soon glittered with pooled serotonin. Serotonergic neurons projected their axons into the amygdale, making us all less emotionally volatile; the hypothalamus, reshaping our sleep patterns; the hippocampus, regulating our ability to remember; and the cerebellum, tuning our attention like radios. How far the government's reach had extended. And no one felt anything but peaceful, perhaps better than they had felt in many years.

Despite the appetite suppressing properties of the powder, the consumption of coffee and pizza increased. As soon as the residual sense of fulfillment wore off, people flocked again to the sources they associated their good feelings with. And like hogs to the truffle, their instincts were consistently accurate. Beer was purchased in even greater quantities, and drunk driving increased eleven-fold. People's hypertension worsened, and cholesterol readings went up in every doctor's office across the nation. Lipitor and Zocor were liberally prescribed.

Sexual activity also dropped, which, in some cases, was a desired side-effect of the doping. Complaints of STDs decreased in urban hospitals, and free clinics likewise reported a dramatic drop in patient numbers. However, more men went to doctors complaining of sexual dysfunction. A cluster of neurons in the hypothalamus was repeatedly failing to open proerectile pathways in the brain, but of course, no one suspected anything unusual at the time. Doctors prescribed Viagra and told them to cut down their caffeine intake and stress levels.

The changes had a particularly egregious downside: in the cities, people began dying. Amazingly, no one had considered what ramifications an increase in serotonin would have for those already taking psychotropic drugs. But perhaps, *perhaps* this was a bit of clandestine eugenics, something that was part of the greater strategic chart for the nation. *Get rid of those defective minds. It will be said that they overdosed, that they committed suicide. We don't need them in our gene pool. The future belongs to the healthiest among us.*

By the end of October, as the last debates aired and the stump speeches began, most of the general population was enjoying the effects of having been medicated for many months. A general feeling of contentment with the status quo had settled over them like a downy quilt, and the incumbent, whom they associated with this sense of well-being and whom they began to admire intensely, sat at the foot of the nation's bed and told this largely unaware, self-concerned brood a fairy-tale about what *had been* and what *would be*. While he was not a master story-teller, in their chemically altered minds, what he said became a certainty.

When the election passed and the incumbent was indeed re-elected, chemical levels abruptly dropped in foods and beverages. It simply cost too much to continue the program. Billions of dollars had been spent to anesthetize the population. The particulars of each deal struck with participating corporations are, apparently, vague, but every one received some reward for their participation, a so-called 'remunerative allowance' for the cost of altering their production methods. But like the water table, the money not retained by savvy lawyers conversant with tax loop holes was simply reabsorbed by that entity which had showered it in the first place. In fact, the government took even more, once profit margins enjoyed a global increase. Still, it was simply not lucrative enough to continue the program. The drug companies supplying the pharmaceutical-grade powders could not continue to meet the new levels of demand, and consequently exacted ever higher prices from federal allocations.

Also at stake was secrecy. To continue the program was to chance exposure and ruin, and the party risked both schism and collapse to secure the results of a single election. Yet never before, they felt, had so much been at issue—a war, an international position. The world was watching with contemptuous eyes. To have power wrested from them then, before things had been brought to a mollifying conclusion, before achieving domination and redemption—two intricately intertwined goals—was unthinkable. Perhaps eight people originally knew the complete truth. And all were considered to be in a position not to speak of it further if questioned. A great deal of deceit, half-truths, and backroom double-dealing was necessary to achieve the outcome.

And apparently, a blissful citizenry was also no longer essential for the theoretical Greater Good. And therefore, we all awoke one mid-November morning much crankier than usual. Our bodies yearned for that which was lacking. Our heads ached. We all collectively perspired. Some of us found our appetites curtailed, while others binged on comfort food, seeking the familiar onset of serenity. Both road rage and murder increased in the months following the nation's united entry into cold turkey. And the following September, a spike in the birth rate occurred. In searching for what was missing, people found an interim placebo. Their carnal desire had returned, unabated.

If we were generous of mind, we might believe that this had begun as a defensive experiment, to determine whether the American population could actually be brought under a collective spell, to find out if the intrinsically dissatisfied human mind could be drawn by artificial means to support an invasive belief system or endorse a previously unpopular political philosophy. But what incredible timing for such an experiment.

Who has said that the satisfied man will not object, much less revolt? The measures and their decisive success had tremendous implications for society's future, for the future of the world. To have an entire population follow you willingly into an unmistakably perilous dawn, that, *that!* is extraordinary, a feat of science and a triumph over free will. Instead of previous generations' indigence and famine, which alters a man's spiritual core, we have split level malls, unwanted possessions, and debt to spur our colorless discontent, a dissatisfaction so bland it inspires no moments of action, only self loathing and fresh consumption. We absently fill ourselves beyond satiety, yet remain eternally unfulfilled. To the politicians, we were not fat and happy, but obese and despondent, obeying Newton's first law of dynamics. The government was the unbalancing force that acted upon us. They set us in motion for their benefit and then laid us again to rest.

How did it work out for us? Oh David and I enjoyed an entirely different perception of reality for a little while. The holes underneath us remained closed. They did not even leak the acrid fragrance we had come to recognize as anxiety, but as we were abruptly and unwittingly weaned of the chemicals, David suffered a collapse. He complained of dizziness and nightmares first, and then suddenly and inexplicably, he began stuttering. Over a period of a few weeks, he went from ebullience tinged with hints of mania to an unresponsiveness punctuated by unexpected outbursts of violence. He had no great amount of money, so he was sent off to St. Elizabeth's, and I have not seen him since.

So how is it that I know everything I've told you? Well, people who know things and shouldn't talk often do. Give a man too many Manhattans at a cocktail party and revelations can flood from his mouth in great bilious rivers. I once had a strange gift for exciting my conversational partners to divulge both the covert and the shocking. I did nothing but nod my head and widen my eyes at appropriate moments, but it always elicited the same confessional responses. Therefore, I gained a great deal of unwanted knowledge. And knowledge, I'm afraid, brings unhappiness. If I were forced to replace it with something, it would be wisdom. Wisdom has the patina of experience to soften its uneven edges. The raw hysteria that follows knowledge, which often comes at me through every sensory faculty, is why I can no longer travel in the outside world. My experiences must now be filtered and regulated. Of course, because of my condition, no one takes me seriously when I tell them what I know. But then, it could be that they are even more medicated than I am. And wouldn't that be funny?

DON SILVER

RESEARCHING FICTION AS A
PARTICIPANT OBSERVER

Don Silver
Researching Fiction as a Participant Observer

WORKSHOP DESCRIPTION

Early in my current novel, I created a character who had a good job and a loving family, but who, it became apparent, was interested in seeing a professional dominatrix. He does this and finds that he likes it. A lot. This kind of thing will happen in fiction: a plot idea or a character will twist out of the experience of the author and into another world, which is when the fun begins. At the same time, fiction depends, in some measure, upon verisimilitude. It doesn't make bad writing good, but it makes good writing better. I want to explore how to do research when what you are writing about is beyond your experience and ability to imagine and not available from the library or the web. There is a practical side, a whimsical side, a challenging side and an entrepreneurial aspect to doing research as well as a personal aspect; namely, how not to risk your marriage or your life. Please bring a gnarly idea or challenging research topic that you are currently facing or expect to be facing in the near future in the form of a character description—the more vexing, the better.

INSTRUCTOR BIOGRAPHY

Don Silver is a Philadelphia. based writer whose first novel, *Backward-Facing Man*, will be released in paperback by Ecco/HarperCollins in the fall of 2006.

CURTIS SITTENFELD

STORY-WRITING 101

Curtis Sittenfeld
Story-Writing 101

WORKSHOP DESCRIPTION

If you've never written a story before, how do you get started? This class is for people who have always wanted to write fiction-and especially those who have a particular idea in mind-but who aren't sure how to get their ideas on paper. We will discuss the basics of structure, plot, character, and language. We'll also examine which of the many clichés about writing (Write what you know! Find your voice!) are worth heeding and which are best ignored.

INSTRUCTOR BIOGRAPHY

Curtis Sittenfeld's first novel, *Prep*, was a national bestseller. It was chosen as one of the Ten Best Books of 2005 by *The New York Times*, it will be translated into twenty-two languages, and its film rights have been optioned by Paramount Pictures. Curtis's non-fiction has appeared in *The New York Times, The Washington Post, The Atlantic Monthly, Salon, Allure, Glamour, Real Simple*, and on public radio's *This American Life*. Her second novel, *The Man of My Dreams*, was published by Random House in May.

REBECCA SKLOOT

REPORTING AND WRITING NARRATIVE JOURNALISM: LEARNING TO SHOW INSTEAD OF TELL

SUPPLEMENTARY MATERIALS:

HANDOUT: QUERYING

Rebecca Skloot
Reporting and Writing Narrative Journalism:
Learning to Show Instead of Tell

WORKSHOP DESCRIPTION

Every story—whether it's a 500-word news piece or a 10,000-word feature—has narrative potential. They've all got characters, action, scenes, and dialogue that writers can use to bring a story to life. The problem is, many writers (especially journalists) are trained to report only for facts, not facts plus narrative. You go out, interview sources and get good quotes, then sit down at your desk and realize, you've got no narrative details, which means your story will be flat (because it's not a*story* at that point, it's a string of facts). Most writers know the phrase "show don't tell." We hear it from teachers and editors, but it's not always clear what that means, or how to accomplish it. "Showing" is all about narrative, and most editors are hungry to work with writers who can pull it off (this is true for newspapers, magazines, radio, television and books). This workshop will teach the secret to writing good narrative, which lies in learning narrative reporting techniques—interviewing, observing, taking specialized notes, fostering an intimate setting that allows your subjects to be themselves, and more. These techniques are key to finding stories, developing characters, and writing good narrative, because no matter how well you string sentences together, if you don't report for narrative, you'll always tell and never show.

INSTRUCTOR BIOGRAPHY

Rebecca Skloot is an award-winning freelance writer, a contributing editor at *Popular Science* magazine, and a television correspondent for PBS's Nova ScienceNOW series. She writes for *The New York Times* and *New York Times Magazine, Discover, New York*, and others. She specializes in narrative journalism and is known to cover a wide range of topics—from food politics and goldfish surgery to packs of wild dogs in Manhattan—but her focus is science. Skloot has contributed chapters and writing exercises to multiple textbooks, and her work has been anthologized several in essay collections, including *The Best Food Writing 2005*. She's on the Board of Directors of the National Book Critics Circle, where she serves as a judge for their yearly book awards, and she teaches at the yearly Mid-Atlantic Summer Creative Nonfiction Writers Conference. Her first book, *The Immortal Life of Henrietta Lacks*, is forthcoming from Crown. For more information, visit her website at *www.rebeccaskloot.com*.

querying by rebecca skloot

(compiled by elaine vitone using handouts by and a phone interview with rebecca skloot)

overview

When I first started freelancing, I was constantly trying to expand my client base, so I sent out a lot of blind queries. It's important to think of a query letter not just as a story pitch, but as a pitch of you and your writing. I've sold many stories this way, and sometimes queries that an editor didn't want still got me work with that magazine: I've had editors reply saying they liked the query but couldn't commission the story for one reason or another, but that they'd like to hear other ideas from me and I didn't have to bother with a whole query next time. From that point on, I queried those editors with a quick email saying, "Would you be interested in a story about blah," and if they said yes, we talked about the idea over the phone. Some of these turned into good relationships where ideas now come from both directions.

Aside from the obvious (the ability to write and a story idea) I think the most important requirements for writing successful queries are persistence, thick skin, pre-query research, more thick skin and more persistence.

Developing the idea and writing the query sounds like more work than it actually is. I got my queries down to a kind of formula, which includes a basic paragraph about who I am and why I should write the story. I cut and paste that, then tinker to fit the publication and story. I often write on related topics, so background information and basics of the story can work via cut-and-paste too.

I used to spend hours and hours doing pre-query research and writing the letter, but after doing that a few times and having the query flop, I decided it was best to not go overboard. I do enough to make sure there's a story there, then if an editor replies with interest, I go back and do more research.

tips

- Don't try to break into every magazine at once. It's a lot more effective to pick one and do a good job with it. Editors know when you're blanket pitching—it's obvious.
- Know the publication so that in your query you can show them that you've done your homework and are right for them. Don't pitch a profile to a magazine that doesn't do profiles; don't pitch a news story to a magazine that does mostly literary or historical stuff.
- Make your blind pitch as far from blind as possible (see "the query letter/email" section, page 3).
- Pitch to an associate, assistant or senior editor instead of the editor-in-chief, executive editor or managing editor, who truly are too busy to read queries from new writers and aren't always as on-the-lookout for new talent.
- Try to have at least two queries in circulation at all times.
- Never let a query sit on your desk for more than a day—once it's been rejected or ignored, pitch it somewhere else, so you always have something out there.
- Don't feel like you *have* to live in New York if you're going to be a writer. Non-New York writers are actually very desirable. Editors depend on them to tell readers what's going on in the rest of the world.
- One way to make connections with editors no matter where you live is to volunteer to organize and moderate panels. Then you get to hand-pick who you want to meet.
- Loyalty really means something to editors. Keep coming back, let them know you're pitching just to them. The fact that you actually know something about the magazine and care about it is important.
- If I'm interviewing somebody, I always let them go off on tangents. New stories often come from digressions in stories I'm already writing.

pre-query research

I recommend never calling an editor. They're busy and fielding phone calls from countless writers and PR people wanting their attention. And, if you call to pitch a story, the only answer they can give you is, Write a pitch and send it—they can't tell whether you can write over the phone. Pitching over the phone makes you appear inexperienced and runs the risk of annoying an editor to the point where he/she won't read your ideas once you send them. If you want to get in touch with an editor you don't know, call the reception desk at the magazine and ask for his or her email address.

I use Internet searches and databases (like Lexis Nexis) to read what's been written on any subject I'm hoping to write about. And I make quadruply sure no one has already written the story I'm pitching (I learned this lesson the hard way after pitching a story to a big national magazine days after the exact story ran in their competitor's magazine, which made me look like an idiot). I do this by reading at least the table of contents and leads from zillions of magazines on a regular basis so I can keep up on what's being covered by which publications. I also ask friends who follow the media, because they'll often know whether my story—or something like it—has been done recently.

I always do a preliminary interview (these are usually very short) to make sure I have access to the story I'm pitching, and to get quotes and character details I can use in the query to (a) show my access and (b) give the pitch some life. since I often get story ideas while doing interviews for other stories, when anything grabs my attention, I'll ask enough questions to find out if there's a story there, which serves as my preliminary interview if I pitch the story in the future. That makes the whole process easier, and much more efficient.

the query letter/email

To make your queries as far from blind as possible, I suggest a three-part approach: First, plant your name in their heads in a short email introducing yourself, saying who you've written for and something about how you know them (either "so-and-so recommended I contact you," or "I saw you speak at Blank Conference, and was struck by what you said about Blah, which inspired me to contact you," or "I read this piece you wrote or edited in *Blah Magazine*, which inspired me to contact you" . . . or something along those lines). From my experience as an editor, and from talking with editors, I say this can help you get in the door without landing in the slushpile.

Second, after introducing yourself and making it clear you've done your homework about the editor and/or the magazine, explain that you have a story idea you think they'd be interested in, and ask how they prefer to receive queries: email, fax, snail mail, etc. In my experience, editors usually respond to this preliminary email within a day or so, because it's easy for them to fire off the information. This is good for several reasons: you don't end up sending a query by email to someone who despises email queries, and most importantly, *you've planted your name in their brains.* Chances are they'll then open your query when you send it (BTW: I can only think of one time an editor didn't respond to say email queries were fine).

Third, write your actual query. Keep in mind that queries aren't just about showing that you have a good idea; they're about making yourself stand out by showing that you can write. Try to keep your actual queries to one page, and structure them as you would structure a story: make sure to have a lead, a nutgraph, and an overall structure to the whole thing (like coming back to the lead in the end, or something like that) to show them you know how to put a story together. The hardest part of the whole thing is usually finding the lead.

It's good to throw at least one line in the query to indicate that you know their magazine and/or audience, like *Since readers of* Blah Magazine *are primarily women of blah age, this story would appeal to them because of blah,* or *Like the story you did last month on Blah, this story will do Blah for you readers* . . . something like that. At the end of my queries, I say if they'd like to see samples of my writing they can do so on my website, which I provide a link to (they often don't look for it in the sig line so I give it in the text of the email). Then I say if they'd like hard copies of clips I'd be happy to send them if they provide me with a mailing address. I've only had one editor reply and ask for hard copies of clips.

following up

The kind of follow-up I do depends on the timeliness of the story. If I'm pitching a story that needs to be acted on quickly, I say so in my query and end with something like, "Given the timely nature of this story, I hope to hear from you soon so I can market it elsewhere if you're not interested." I've found this to be effective, partially because editors are people too and it's good to remind them that you're trying to make a living, and also (I think) because it gives a hint of competition, like if they don't grab it someone else will, but that may just be in my head.

On a timely story, if I haven't heard back in a week (or a few days, depending on the story), I'll send an email saying I wanted to check to see if they got it, and I'll paste my original email at the bottom so they don't have to go digging for it. (The more you can do to show an editor you understand and respect how busy they are, the better) If I don't hear after a week (maybe less, depending on the story), then I'll call. If I call and get no reply, then I move on to another publication and don't waste my time with that editor any more. If it's a less pressing story, I'll give them several weeks to reply (this is usually about four weeks—my rule of thumb is, resist the temptation to nag an editor until you can't stand it any more, then wait another week). Then I follow a similar path (email, call, move on).

Usually the follow-up email gets some response, even if it's a simple "We're not interested." Don't follow up on these to try to find out why they weren't interested, just send it to someone else.

strategies for breaking into national markets

start with institutional publications

One of the best ways to get started with writing in any area, especially science writing, is alumni magazines. The pay is good, and they often give writers the space and freedom to develop stories that can really show writing style. Almost every major university has an alumni magazine, most have more than one: usually the medical school has its own magazine, as do the schools of public health, business, etc. You can usually find them by doing a little research online, or contacting university public relations offices. Oftentimes these magazines have their own story ideas that they use with freelancers, but it doesn't hurt to have a story in mind when you contact them. If you're located in another country, your best bet is to find an American scientist who's doing interesting work, then find out what university he/she went to, and pitch a story about that person to their alma mater. Alumni magazines are a great way to get clips, but they're also a perfect way to get into labs where cutting-edge research is being done, which provides material you can then pitch to national magazines. Also, as a way of paying the bills while freelancing, writing for public relations offices can be a very good thing. They hire freelancers to write newsletters, guidebooks, press releases, you name it.

pitch a book review

Book reviews are a great way to break in. Book-review assignments are much easier to get because the pay is awful, and there's not as much riding on it for the editor. (If you turn in a review and it doesn't work, they just rewrite it or don't run it. Their production schedule doesn't usually depend on it.) I started with *The San Francisco Chronicle*. The day my first review ran, I emailed the editor of *The Chicago Tribune* book section to pitch a review, introducing myself as a reviewer for *The San Francisco Chronicle*, even though I only had one clip. I got that assignment, then the day it ran, I turned around and pitched *The Boston Globe* saying, I review for *The San Francisco Chronicle* and *Chicago Tribune*. I kept repeating that until I had five national publications on my bio from only five reviews. My motto: If you've got one clip from a publication, say "I write for *Blah Publication*." Who cares if you've only done one review. So much of breaking in has to do with having the guts to be the writer you want to be.

be curious

The key to breaking into the national market is having good original ideas to pitch—these don't come from press releases, they come from living life as a writer. Find ideas no one else has. Notice everything around you, follow every curious statement and bend in the road as if it might lead to a story. My favorite example of this is the story I did on fish medicine for *The New York Times Magazine*. I was at the vet with my dog; a doctor came into the room pulling off his exam gloves, and another vet asked how his surgery went. His response: "Great, patient's up, swimming around." I walked across the room and said, "Excuse me, did you say your patient is swimming?" I proceeded to interview him about fish surgery for nearly an hour with my dog standing next to me while I scribbled notes on my vet bill. Don't be afraid to eavesdrop and be curious. talk to strangers, follow your instincts.

get clips

Once you have good story ideas, the other key is good writing samples to back them up. If you can't get freelance work or a paid staff position for any reason (such as missing clips), magazines are usually happy to take interns on a volunteer basis. Doing that for a short period of time is a good way to break in and start getting the necessary experience and clips to move forward. Also, a well-written query letter can serve as a good writing sample. And finally, writers today are fortunate: If you don't have clips, you can make your own if you . . .

start a blog

Write little stories once a week and viola, you've started your own magazine. Editors I know are happy to look at blogs as clips—in fact, I know many who prefer it, because there's no editor changing your work, so they can see how you really write, which isn't always the case with published clips. (And, on a cautionary note, editors *do* look at blogs, so make sure the stuff you're blogging is stuff you'd want an editor to see and judge your writing by. Don't treat it casually.) Before jumping in to blogging, read several by writers you respect to see how they're doing it and to come up with a style of your own.

post your own site

Having your own web site helps. I put a link to mine at the bottom of all my emails. People usually click because they're curious. It shows editors that you're serious and makes your clips easily available. Eventually people find you and seek you out because of your site. It's also useful when I contact people hoping to write about them—it shows I'm legit and gives them a way to get to know me a bit. Ditto for a blog. (Again, be careful: people you contact wanting to write about them will Google you and find your blog. So make sure your blog postings are in keeping with the way you want both your editors and potential sources to see you.)

be brave

Much of a writer's success has to do with having the guts to just walk up to an editor and say, "Hi. I'm a writer. I'm gonna email you sometime." Then you contact them, say you met at conference, that you liked what they had to say on a panel discussion, or in a presentation. Have the moxie to call editors whether you've met them or not, ask them to lunch, show them that you have the enthusiasm do whatever it takes for a story.

use the buddy system

It's very important to have a network of writers you can depend on. My friends and I send each other stuff all the time. I know what they like to write about, and vice versa. We help each other keep up with the reading ("Oh my God, did you see the piece on blah? You've got to read this!). One of my best friends is a wonderful writer I met in grad school—he and I read every one of our big magazine stories out-loud to each other over the phone as we write them (we've been known to talk more than 12 times in a day, sometimes calling to read each section of a story as we write it if we need feedback). We also read every finished piece before we submit them to our editors. This is invaluable. It's also good to just get together and whine, because writing is hard. You help each other through it. Both psychologically and financially. The freelance mantra: Never turn down work because you never know how long you'll have to go between assignments, but if something comes your way that you can't possibly do, you pass it on to a friend whose writing you know and trust, and they'll do the same for you.

organize

For people interested in science writing, I suggest getting involved with the National Association of Science Writers. Among other things, they have several email listservs that are an amazing resources (for members and nonmembers). Two, which are called NASW-freelance and NASW-talk are great ways to network and meet other science writers (both established and beginners), and editors, who often pass work on to each other. Make sure to look at all the online tips for beginning science writers, and peruse the list archives before diving in and asking the list, "How do I become a science writer?" since that question has been answered at length on NASW's site. You can find a lot of helpful information in the list archives. Another list, NASW-jobs, is essentially a job board that sends out announcements of magazines needing employees and/or freelancers, and places looking to make staff hires. You can check out NASW's website at *www.nasw. org*. There's a job board page on there (I don't think you need to be a member to peruse it), and there's also a link to NASW's freelance site, which is full of helpful information.

If you're interested in something other than science writing, there are plenty of other similar organizations you'll find helpful: The National Writers Union (*www.nwu.org*), the American Society of Journalists and Authors (*www.asja.org* . . . My personal favorite) has a wonderful online community, which is great for meeting other writers and editors, and they do one of the best annual conferences (it's in NYC every year in April, full of great editors and writers). The National Book Critics Circle (*www.bookcritics.org*) has a similar community.

read up on the biz

As an online resource, with links to sites for research, copyright information, finding grants, and everything between, you can visit the "Links" page of my website at *www.rebeccaskloot.com*.

###

CARLA SPATARO

POLISHING YOUR FICTION FOR PUBLICATION

SUPPLEMENTARY MATERIALS:

HANDOUT: TEN BASIC RULES FOR POLISHING SHORT FICTION

Carla Spataro
Polishing Your Fiction for Publication

WORKSHOP DESCRIPTION

Have you been sending out your work, but have been getting nothing but rejection slips? Don't worry, you're in good company. Most writers' rejection slips far out-weigh their acceptances. In this workshop we will discuss ten rules for good writing with an emphasis on self-editing and polishing, as well as the dos and don'ts of the submission process.

INSTRUCTOR BIOGRAPHY

C.J. Spataro is a 2005 Pennsylvania Council on the Arts Fellowship recipient. Her work has been both a finalist and won second place in the Philadelphia City Paper Fiction contest and she has had two stories presented at the InterAct Theatre's Writing Aloud. Her short fiction can be read in *Wild River Review, XConnect* and *Hackwriters.com*. Currently, she is the fiction editor and co-publisher of *Philadelphia Stories Magazine*.

TEN BASIC RULES FOR POLISHING SHORT FICTION BY CARLA SPATARO

Before you've crafted the perfect cover letter, found and corrected every typo, made sure that you've adhered to every specific request in the guidelines, comes the biggest challenge of all—is your story any good?

1. BE WILLING TO BE RUTHLESS

In order to create the best story possible you must be willing to revise, rewrite and cut. It doesn't matter if it's your favorite character, phrase, subplot or setting—if it's not propelling the story forward or supporting character development it needs to go!

2. KNOW YOUR AUDIENCE

Regardless of the age of the main character is this story for adults or are the themes better suited for young adults or children? (For example: A story of a Grandmother explaining the wonders of Christmas to her granddaughter might be better suited for a young adult journal than a literary journal). If a journal says they don't publish science fiction, then don't waste their time by sending them your story about Mars. Know who you're writing for and what they want to read.

3. IS MY STORY UNDER-FICTIONALIZED?

Okay, so you've based your short story on something that's happened to you or someone you know. Everyone does this, but does the story read like a personal essay or does it feel like a fully realized piece of fiction? Stories that feel under-fictionalized are usually unsatisfying. Sometimes something as simple as changing the point of view from first to third person can help take a piece from "What I Did on my Summer Vacation" to a story about two friends who find a secret swimming hole and discover something new about their relationship. Changing the names of your characters, the location or even the sex of the protagonist can help "fictionalize" your real-life inspired story.

4. POINT OF VIEW—IS THIS THE RIGHT POINT OF VIEW FOR MY STORY?

First person is the easiest to control for most beginning writers but is it really the right perspective for my piece?

Third person limited gives the author more psychic distance and a chance to observe all the characters more objectively, but do you need to be more inside the head of the main character?

Third person omniscient, the most difficult to control, gives the author access to the thoughts of all the characters but if not handled properly can be extremely confusing.

Second person, the most "experimental" puts the reader directly into the story, but again can be very difficult to control if not handled properly.

Ask yourself as the author, am I in control of the point of view, or is it in control of me?

5. OVERUSE OF METAPHORS AND CLICHES

A few creatively placed, well thought out metaphors can add a great deal to a story and be fun to write but using clichés is always a bad idea. (The best exception to this is of course in dialog. The use of bad metaphors and clichés in dialog can be telling and humorous if done well.)

6. ADVERBS

Use sparingly or not at all. This is really important. Overuse of adverbs is just plain lazy! If an editor reads more than one or two carefully placed adverbs in a story, especially when attached to a dialog tag (she said desperately) then they will know that the author is not working as hard as they should. The character's emotional state and intent must be made plain through dialog, action and description.

7. ADJECTIVES, ELEVATED VOCABULARY AND LONG FLOWERY SENTENCES

Have you gone thesaurus crazy? Are your sentences carefully crafted with varied vocabulary and varied length? Or are they overly long and convoluted in an attempt to show the reader what a great writer you are? In an attempt to punch up your prose are you using the right verbs? Plopping down into a chair can be very descriptive, but sometimes sitting is just sitting. Make sure that the verbs that you use are appropriate to the mood you are trying to create and that your nouns and adjectives are direct and concrete.

8. STUDY UP AND LEARN YOUR CRAFT

Read the basics: Start with the classic, The Art of Fiction, by John Gardner—pay particular attention to chapters five and six—there is invaluable information here for writer's at any level. Then move on to Strunk & White, William Zinzer's *On Writing Well, Bird by Bird*, by Anne Lamott, On Writing by Stephen King—and many, many more. You must understand grammar basics as a foundation for any writing. It's fine to break the rules, but you need to understand them first.

Join or start a writer's group with readers you trust: It's frightening to share your work with others, but this is a necessary step to identifying your strengths and weaknesses (character, voice, plot, narrative, etc.). No good published author works in a vacuum. It's just too hard to critique yourself. **You do *not* want a magazine to be your first reader**.

Read, read, read—television and movies are entertaining, but they cannot take the place of reading a book. If you're not interested in reading how will you know what else is out in the marketplace?

Find appropriate online and print magazines for your work.

In print: Writer's Marketplace
Council of Literary Magazines and Presses: *www.clmp.org*
Publisher's Lunch: www.publisherslunch.com

The O. Henry Prize: *http://www.randomhouse.com/anchor/ ohenry*

Duotrope Digest: www.duotrope.com

9. FOLLOW GUIDELINES.

I cannot stress this enough. Does the magazine accept only online submissions? Only Word format? Do you need to include a bio? Read the guidelines carefully and thoroughly before sending anything out. Anything less is unprofessional.

Here are the basics: In the upper left or right-hand corner (single spaced):

    Name
    Address
    Phone
    Email
    Word Count

Next, centered on the page is the Title. Indent your paragraphs and dialog. DO NOT double the double space. You are writing a short story, not a business letter. You do not need a cover page. Use one inch margins. Include page numbers in the header or the footer—along with your name—unless you are requested not to for the purposes of a contest. Use a 12 point font, either Courier or Times New Roman and double space. DO NOT send out double sided copies. DO NOT staple—you can use a paper clip. And if requested include a SASE with the appropriate postage.

IF you send a cover letter make it clear, concise, and targeted toward the specific magazine to which you are sending. KEEP IT SHORT! DO NOT summarize the story—I want to read it for myself. DO NOT send what you think is a witty or cryptic note. DO NOT tell me how great you are and list all the reasons why I should publish your story. DO NOT send a complete list of all previous publications along with titles of the stories. DO NOT send a curriculum vitae. DO

NOT send newspaper clippings about yourself or your writing, copies of previously published materials or photos of yourself!

Send out *only* polished material.

Editors remember names. You want to make a positive first impression.

10. ACCEPT REJECTION WITH DIGNITY.

Just because your piece isn't right for one publication doesn't mean it's bad. Selection is an extremely subjective process. DO NOT under any circumstances send the editor a rebuttal, a rebuke or antagonize them in any way. You may feel better for a few minutes but any hope that you ever had of seeing your work in that journal is now gone FOREVER. Use rejection as an opportunity to send out more work.

If an editor asks for a rewrite, take it seriously. If he or she offers specific feedback, value that response. It generally means that they thought your piece had potential and may publish it after a second look.

ERIN STALCUP

LINKED SHORT-STORIES: PRODUCING NEW WORK THROUGH INTERCONNECTION

Erin Stalcup
Linked Short-Stories: Producing New Work Through Interconnection

WORKSHOP DESCRIPTION

Are you unsure of how to build your finished stories into a full-length collection? Are you struggling to get ideas for new work? Alternatively, do you have a group of stories that aren't quite satisfying to you, but you're at a loss for how to revise? Interconnected short stories might give you energy and ideas for both revision and generation. This class will look at different ways collections of short stories have been linked, both completely and partially. We will discuss practical ways that you can tie together stories that you already have written, and we will focus on how to take one story you have that is "finished," and use the idea of interconnection to generate new, coordinated stories. In addition, we will discuss the marketing benefits of interconnected stories. To participate in this class, please e-mail me a short story that you are satisfied with (it doesn't have to be "done," the class will produce suggestions for revision, but it should be a story you feel good about, where you have a good grip on the characters and the plot). I will offer suggestions for revision, as well as mine the story in order to find nuggets of future linked stories. In addition, I will pick approximately 3 stories that I think will produce good discussion, e-mail them to the class, and we will workshop them as a group, looking for ways which the stories might branch out into others. My goal is to have everyone leave the class with a project, a plan for 1-3 specific future stories to work on. You will be required to e-mail me a story (10 pages maximum) no later than two weeks before the conference (before October 1). When you enroll in the workshop, you will receive instructions on where and how to email your story. I will e-mail you the three stories we will workshop together no later than a week before the conference (October 7).

INSTRUCTOR BIOGRAPHY

Erin Stalcup is from Flagstaff, Arizona but currently lives in Brooklyn. She teaches at a community college in Washington Heights, a Dominican neighborhood in Manhattan. Her fiction has appeared in *Puerto del Sol* and is forthcoming in the *Seattle Review*, and she was a finalist for *Glimmer Train's* Very Short Fiction Award. She is currently at work on a novel-in-stories, entitled *Trees Breathe*.

DUANE SWIERCZYNSKI

WRITING FOR ALT-NEWSWEEKLIES

Duane Swierczynski
Writing For Alt-Newsweeklies

WORKSHOP DESCRIPTION

Some of the most exciting and experimental writing is being done in the alternative newsweeklies, and this workshop is designed to help students break into the rapidly growing field. First, we will discuss how alt-weeklies conceive and execute their ideas. Next, we will talk about generating ideas that no self-respecting alt-weekly editor could possibly refuse, followed by sure-fire ways to pitch them. Finally, we'll talk about how to keep that editor-writer relationship alive and well, so that your first assignment is never your last.

INSTRUCTOR BIOGRAPHY

Duane Swierczynski is the editor-in-chief of the *Philadelphia City Paper* and the author of The Wheelman (St. Martin's Minotaur), which has been optioned by Plum Films. This fall, *The Blonde*, his third crime thriller, will be published. He's also the author of *Secret Dead Men* (PointBlank Press) and six non-fiction books about vice and crime, including *The Big Book O' Beer* (Quirk Books). A Philly native, Swierczynski has worked as an editor at *Details, Men's Health and Philadelphia Magazine*, and has taught journalism at his alma mater, La Salle University. Check out his blog and website at *www. duaneswierczynski.com.*

CAROLINE TIGER

BREAKING IN: HOW TO PITCH MAGAZINES

Caroline Tiger
Breaking In: How To Pitch Magazines

WORKSHOP DESCRIPTION

It is difficult to snag a writing assignment without already having a portfolio of clips. So how are you supposed to get your first, second and third clips? It is not as daunting as it might seem. How many magazines can you think of off the top of your head? There are probably 50 major magazines—these are the ones you see on the newsstand at Barnes & Noble—but there are more than 10,000 magazines published in America. We'll learn about the wide scope of opportunities that exists for magazine writers and we'll cover the basics of querying: what makes a story idea good, where to look for story ideas, how to match those ideas with appropriate markets, and how to write professional query letters that stand a chance of surviving an editor's circular file. This workshop is for beginners, but intermediates might also learn something new.

INSTRUCTOR BIOGRAPHY

Caroline Tiger is a graduate of the University of Pennsylvania (class of '96) and a former Managing Editor of *Philadelphia* magazine. During the three years she's been freelancing, her work has appeared in many national publications including *Self, Good Housekeeping, Men's Health, Marie Claire, Salon, Ms.*, and *Town and Country*. She has also authored several books, including *The Long-Distance Relationship Guide: Advice for the Geographically Challenged* and *How To Behave: A Guide to Modern Manners for the Socially Challenged*. She lives in Philadelphia and can be found online at *www.carolinetiger.com*.

JOHN TIMPANE

WRITING FOR THE OP-ED PAGE

SUPPLEMENTARY MATERIALS:

ARTICLE: *WHY CAN'T WE BE FRIENDS?*

John Timpane
Writing for the Op-Ed Page

WORKSHOP DESCRIPTION

Writing for the Op-Ed page is an enjoyable but exacting art. You need to have a clear point of view. You must hit the reader's mind running, stay concrete, avoid abstraction, and express your views in a personal, stylish manner. And it's all over in 700 words. We'll look at successful Op-Ed pieces (and un-) and try our hands at writing and critiquing them.

INSTRUCTOR BIOGRAPHY

John Timpane is editor of the Commentary Page of *The Philadelphia Inquirer*. Previously he was an English professor at Stanford, Rutgers, and Lafayette College as well as a freelance writer and his opinion, essays, reviews and perspective pieces have appeared in numerous papers. He also co-authored *Writing Worth Reading* (Bedford, 1994) and *It Could Be Verse* (Berkeley: Ten Speed, 1995) with Nancy H. Packer, and *Poetry for Dummies* (Hungry Minds, 2000) with Maureen Watts.

Philadelphia Inquirer
Dec 18, 2005

Why Can't We Be Friends?

Friendship across gender requires trust, loyalty, acknowledgment and work. That ideal shouldn't be so difficult to attain.

By John Timpane

Can men and women be friends?

The world says: No!

Aristotle, puzzling the matter out in Books 8 and 9 of the Nicomachean Ethics, decided that, although married people and former lovers may attain something like friendship, it can't be the highest kind, that based on character. The relationship will inevitably be based on pleasure instead.

Literature, philosophy—nearly barren of such friendships. Not until the last 30 years has any real discussion arisen—most of it, alas, either skeptical or, in the case of the social sciences, pretty confused.

The obstacles, people say, are too great. They quote Billy Crystal, playing Harry Burns in When Harry Met Sally: "Men and women can't be friends—because the sex part always gets in the way."

One hears the ambient cliche of the "gay man friend" who offers a woman the companionship of a male without the hazards. Folks bemoan the obstacles to trust (see "the sex part," above). Manipulative! cries each gender, pointing to the other. Competition for scarce resources! (So that's what people think: Gender relations as remorseless jungle competition!)

Distressing. For it implies that roughly half the world's people cannot be friends with the other half. Such a calamity that I choose not to believe it.

This isn't the only kind of friendship we need to work on. One could name friendship across races, classes, or generations. But let me propose the following: Friendship between men and women can be the highest kind, that based on character. (Aristotle? Well, that was then.) If pursued mindfully and with compassion, friendships across gender can be very rewarding precisely because they require special kinds of work, continual maintenance, to create and maintain trust. They can be very durable because, being across genders, they must be based on more than "what we have in common." Friends across genders will always be negotiating difference, learning a new world, a new way to see. They learn to come out of themselves, assume a third view, a new third thing.

To improve at such friendships, we'd have to change much about how we think and act. It can be done. And should be: In the coming decades, our society could hardly undertake a worthier project than the cultivation and celebration of friendship across gender.

There is a payoff, too—one that can enlarge our worlds.

Am I wrong, or is cross-gender friendship more common among people 17 to 30? My generation (40 and up) never was better than uneasy with it. But young adults, many of them, at least, are easier. They report that sometimes it's real ("Sure, men and women can be friends.") and sometimes phony ("They pretend to, but the game's the same."). I hope they're making inroads.

Let's take a cue from them and imagine a plan for 21st-century friendship, a mind-set men and women might adopt to make friendship more likely. (Some qualifiers here. Not "everybody can be friends." They can't and shouldn't try. Friendship is not always smooth; on the contrary, it will ebb and swell with the fortunes of life. Nor is it realistic to expect that friends always are or should be dead-equal. There will be leaders and followers, dominants and submissives.)

Acknowledgment. This is the most important thing one friend can give another. It's a skill, and we can get better at it, with practice. I actually see you. Full rights, full standing. This takes listening, patience, learning about the other's world. Friends remember what the other says and does and thinks. We carry the image of our friends with us—because we think they deserve it, because we like thinking about them, because they carry us where they go.

Safety and freedom. Closely related to acknowledgment. With me, you are accepted as you are. I accept you—and you, me. Friends do not try to mold the other into something else, conform them to a pre-existing agenda. Not that friends never disagree—that is inevitable and healthy. Many friends hold different views, lead different lives. But friends should be able to be vulnerable in each other's presence, to share doubt, conflict, difficulty. If not, they are acquaintances, not friends.

We don't set our friends completely free. Friendship creates the obligation to speak if something is wrong, to respond if something is asked, to intervene when it's called for. To echo Alice Walker, "No one is your friend who demands your silence."

Disinterest. Not uninterest, but disinterest. I am friends with you for your own sake, not for the sake of something I can get from our connection. Not that friendships never involve gain or advantage. But if gain is my main motive for friendship, then it isn't friendship.

Solidarity. Friends support each other, take each other's part. When there is suffering and trouble, friends go to each other. I like the current slang phrase, "We're solid." Two friends make a new, third thing greater than either alone.

Trust and loyalty. Related to solidarity. I can depend on my friend and she on me. All that is promised will be delivered; all that is secret will stay secret. She doesn't have to worry; neither do I.

Trust is something earned rather than awarded. Friends perform the labor of friendship; willing to give up time and work, they assay certain risks for the sake of the friendship. As she works, I work. We create an antiphony of tasks, in fulfilling which we tend this organic, changing entity.

"You haven't mentioned love or gratitude." No—but with the requirements above, do I have to? Who wouldn't love, and be grateful to, a person who accorded them safety, freedom, disinterested solidarity, trust, and loyalty?

Old mind-set, new time. I've been toying with rehabilitating—this is going to sound corny, but I mean it—the notion of brotherhood and sisterhood. Think of the understanding, tolerance and solidarity brothers and sisters have. There is an element of home in friendship, an echo of family. Why else do some call their friends "homey"? Friendships evoke the ease and openness associated with home, the place where I can be accepted as myself.

In Robert Frost's "Death of the Hired Man," one speaker says that "'home is the place where, when you have to go there, / They have to take you in.'" And another replies: "'I should have called it / Something you somehow haven't to deserve.'" Both have part of it right.

But here's the twist. We should see our friends as our brothers and sisters within a dysfunctional family in a provoking world. Often it's seen that when a family is having trouble, the siblings ally. They sense they need one another. The human race is a family, all right—a family that cannot solve its problems. We are sprinting toward a future that will become only more complex.

Not worse—I actually think it will continue to get better for a greater and greater number (and proportion) of all the world's people. But the problems are going to be big, puzzling, distressing, and we as individuals will need friends. Since mom and dad can't help us, maybe our brothers and sisters can.

Siblinghood has its challenges, of course; the worst fights are intra-familial. But the great challenge is for men and women to discover ways of being brothers and sisters. Can we accept? Can men and women treat each other as people to be known rather than taken or possessed? Can we offer ourselves as home for others?

Our futures would benefit inestimably if we could.

The Payoff. What might such friendships produce that is so precious? Cross-gender friendships involve the sexual recombination of spirits. Difference makes us work: Each friend must labor to make his or her world available to the other, and each must learn to listen to the story of a world he or she doesn't inhabit. That will do more than break down the cluelessness each gender complains of in the other. That will teach us and hone our powers of compassion.

A nascent, grudging, fits-and-starts cooperation between men and women has arisen in the last 50 years, but I want and believe in something more: an expansion of the possibilities; new combinations, new ideas. A world different from yet embracing the woman's world and the man's world.

The future of the planet depends on such friendships. Friendship produces the new third thing, the transcendent entity. It suggests an ethics, a way to do business, a guide for diplomacy, a motive for art, a reason for ourselves to continue and to want others to continue. In short, a way to build a future.

Contact John Timpane at 215-854-4406 or jt@phillynews.com.

ALLISON WHITTENBERG

**BEYOND HARRY POTTER:
CREATING MEMORABLE AND ENDURING
CHARACTERS FOR MIDDLE GRADE AND
YOUNG ADULT READERS**

Allison Whittenberg
Beyond Harry Potter:
Creating Memorable And Enduring Characters For
Middle Grade And Young Adult Readers

WORKSHOP DESCRIPTION

Have you ever been tempted to write a book but were unsure of how to begin? Or perhaps you've tried and tried, but you quickly became stuck. This class will provide valuable tools and techniques to jump-start your work. You'll discover techniques to generate fresh ideas, create memorable characters, and develop plotlines. This will be a craft oriented session suitable for anyone interested in fiction writing. Please bring the first three pages of a work in progress and any questions you may have.

INSTRUCTOR BIOGRAPHY

Allison Whittenberg is the author of two novels, *Sweet Thang* (middle grade) and the upcoming *Life Is Fine* (young adult) both published by Random House/Delacorte. Many of her poems and short stories have appeared in various literary magazines such as *Columbia* and *Meridians*.

MEREDITH SUE WILLIS

BEGINNING YOUR NOVEL

SUPPLEMENTARY MATERIALS:

ARTICLES: *ON CUTTING*
HOW SHE CHOSE THE DAY

Meredith Sue Willis
Beginning Your Novel

WORKSHOP DESCRIPTION

Bring to this workshop an idea that you think would make a good novel. Maybe you once wrote a short story that seemed to demand more development, or perhaps there is an incident or a period from your life that seems to contain infinite possibilities for fictionalizing. Maybe, like Tolstoy, you have long been fascinated by a newspaper clipping that might lead you to a novel—one led him to Anna Karenina. Novels can grow from any seed, but bring one idea to this workshop, and keep it in your mind as we talk about process versus product, plot versus architectonics, summary and scene, and other terms. You will experiment with assignments that can become drafts of several important scenes from the novel-in-your mind. The in-class exercises may include exploring character through place and the senses; using some techniques from film to imagine your story; structuring a scene around dialogue; exposing character through monologue; and experimenting with physical space and physical action. All exercises are meant to be potential passages of the novel you are beginning.

INSTRUCTOR BIOGRAPHY

Meredith Sue Willis is a native of West Virginia who has lived in the Northeast for more than thirty years. Her fourteen published books of fiction and nonfiction include *Dwight's House and Other Stories, Oradell at Sea,* and *Personal Fiction Writing.*

Her first collection of short stories, *In the Mountains of America,* was praised by the *New York Times Book Review* as providing "a[n] . . . important lesson on the nature and function of literature itself."

Her books for children include *Billie of Fish House Lane, The Secret Super Powers of Marco* and *Marco's Monster*, which was named one of *Instructor Magazine's* best books of 1997. The *Harvard Educational Review* called *Personal Fiction Writing* "a terrific resource for the classroom teacher as well as the novice writer."

A Distinguished Teaching Artist of the New Jersey State Council on the Arts from 2000 to 2003, she presently teaches novel writing at New York University and gives workshops in schools in New Jersey. She is also an anti-racism activist in her local community and a four-season organic gardener. Her website is at *http://www.meredithsuewillis.com.*

(first published, BIGCITYLIT, http://www.nycbigcitylit.com/sep2001/ contents/Articles.html)

On Cutting
by Meredith Sue Willis

The best time for making changes in texture and diction in prose writing is after you have drafted several times and decided you are well on your way to a finished piece. This is the time—after you've struggled with your point of view and the order of your scenes and what you are really discovering and revealing and how it all comes out—to spend long hours agonizing over whether to use "red" or "crimson" or "incarnadine."

I don't believe that there is always only one right way of saying something. There are certain short poems of Emily Dickinson's that seem perfect to me, but often the best way to convey the idea varies with the writing situation. For example, I was asked to shorten my sentences when I was editing my first novel for children, The Secret Super Powers of Marco. My first reaction was horror. But then, after enjoying my righteous indignation for a while, it occurred to me that I was writing this book especially for children who don't like to read. I really did want to make my story accessible for as many of them as possible. So I shortened the sentences. I didn't change the words, only put periods where I had had semi-colons. It felt fine.

On my own, with no editors making suggestions, I often cut a really terrific word or image and replace it with a more ordinary one because the terrific image seems to draw too much attention to itself and slows down the reader. Other times, of course, I do the opposite: I come up with a word that really is a show-stopper, because at that moment I actually want to stop the show.

Word choice is, of course, part of the nuts and bolts of writing. I like it best when the word choice follows naturally with the other elements of deep revision, such as adding more specific information or figuring out what voice will tell your story best. However, there are many times when looking directly at the words themselves will open up new insights for revision. Consider the following two lines:

"crazed like the rivulets under the glaze of an old piece of pottery" versus "crazed like the cracks under the glaze of old pottery."

By changing a fancy word (rivulets) to a simpler one (cracks) and cutting a few words ("an old piece of pottery" becomes "old pottery"), the sentence is shorter, easier to visualize (because it has fewer elements), and easier to read aloud. Usually I recommend greater specificity—a particular green Mexican cup, say, rather than just pottery in general—but here we are talking about elements in a simile where too much elaboration is distracting. I wanted that pottery to be just a brief hint of a mental image. 'Rivulets'—a very pretty word—calls too much attention to itself: you begin to think about water and the relative size of a creek and a brook when what I wanted was to describe something that exists in its own right and isn't even wet.

For me, the cutting, polishing, editing, and critiquing are both hard work and great pleasure. This is the time to step back from the work and narrow the eye to make sure it is presenting its best side. But polishing can also be a time for final insights into the material, particularly in writing poetry. For prose writers, the point about how trimming intensifies expression is especially applicable. If I'm writing a short story, between the first full draft and the final version, I typically cut away about a third of the words. Thus, if a short story draft is twenty-five pages of typed manuscript, the final version ends up being around seventeen pages or even fifteen or thirteen. I try to go through my piece (after it has sat for a while) as if I were an easily bored reader, looking for anything that doesn't make the piece more interesting. I try to pretend that someone else wrote all those words and I cut everything that doesn't seem absolutely essential.

TRY THIS: To look closely at your words, try revising by reading backwards, that is, read the last paragraph first, then read the next to the last paragraph, and so on. This gives you an opportunity to get a sense of your paragraphs and sentences as individual entities. Do your sentences stand alone? They may not. After all, everything that comes before leads up to that final sentence, but you are likely to catch repetitious or awkward phrasings that you missed in the forward flow of reading.

TRY THIS: Do a final read-through at as close to your normal reading pace as possible. Don't read at your desk or on your computer screen, but rather, from a hard copy while sitting in your easy chair or in bed or wherever you usually read. Try not to become an editor, but stay a reader. Anything that bothers you or stops you may well be something that would bother or stop another reader. Here is an example of the way I make cuts in my fiction. First is a short passage from a *Dwight's House and Other Stories* (Hamilton Stone Editions, 2004). Susan and Dwight are married; their daughter, Fern, is a teenager, and Susan's father hasn't been answering his phone:

EARLIER VERSION (probably the sixth or seventh version):

> When Susan walked back into the living area, she said, "He isn't answering."
> "He's in the shop fixing something," said Dwight.
> Susan said, "On Sunday morning?"
> "Then maybe he went to church," said Dwight.
> "Oh sure," said Fern. "Grandpa's in church all right."
> "You never know," said Dwight, "you never know when these old sinners are going to repent."

TRIMMED-DOWN VERSION:

> When Susan walked back into the living area, she said, "He isn't answering."
> "Maybe he went to church," said Dwight.
> "Oh sure," said Fern. "Grandpa's in church all right."
> "You never know," said Dwight, "you never know when these old sinners are going to repent."

The earlier version was not bad; in fact, it was perfectly acceptable, and perhaps even more naturalistic than the second since people usually say more words and make more noises and gestures in real life than we conventionally transcribe in writing. In reading this tiny snippet, you may prefer the longer version. In the context of the whole passage, however, I found that tightening the scene helped to emphasize a characteristic of Susan's—that she is laconic, indeed depressed. So the tightening actually does two things at once: it intensifies the scene and adds information about a character.

If you have any doubt about whether a sentence or dialogue exchange should be cut, ask yourself whether it is doing more than one thing at once. If it isn't, it is a likely candidate for cutting.

Perhaps the single most important technique for revising is the simplest: Get a distance on your writing. Separate the process from the product. Imagine the reader reading it. Imagine the toughest English teacher you ever had going over it. And if you have trouble getting distance on it, lay it aside for six months, one month, a week, a day.

TRY THIS: As an experiment, take some short passage of your writing (a page, a long paragraph) and set yourself the task of reducing the length by one-third. Be very strict with yourself. Can you do it?

TRY THIS: Try the same exercise, exchanging pieces with a friend. Try to pare down the other person's piece by one-third or one-half. Is it easier or harder to work on someone else's piece?

TRY THIS: Just as hearing your work by reading it aloud or tape recording it can give you the extra distance to edit better, so can the physical relationship of your eyes to the words. If you work on a computer, print out a hard copy, and revise on that for a while, or if you are working on a manuscript, carry it to a higher table and work on it in a standing position for a while, so that your eyes quite literally have a different perspective, a different distance. If you are working at a computer, push your chair back so that you are farther from the screen and keyboard.

There is an old cartoon in which a sculptor has a visitor in his studio. The sculptor is working at a great multi-ton chunk of marble; the visitor's question, though not stated, is obvious. "Oh," says the sculptor, "I just chip away everything that doesn't look like an elephant." I don't know how good the joke is, but the lesson for a writer is excellent: if it isn't a part of this particular elephant—or story or poem or essay or book or even of this line or phrase—chip it away.

But I would also add, save the chips. Taking something away is not the same as destroying it, nor is it the same as saying the first version was bad or a failure. Those rejected words may have been vital to your process of working through your piece. Or, they may have been part of an idea that underlies your present idea but has been superseded.

Most importantly, they may be the beginning of something new.

*(Short short story, first published, BIGCITYLIT, http://www.nycbigcitylit.
com/jul2001/contents/Fiction.html)*

How She Chose the Day
By Meredith Sue Willis

The first day had heavy air and row after row of greasy clouds. The second day had a high sky, painfully fresh, after much heat and dampness. It was a day when distances were precise and the white clarity of edges like a high-pitched baby's cry.

The cry turned to keening, her sons were dead again, her husband had betrayed her again, and the work she had thought might sustain had failed. Courage to go on was beside the point; she had nothing to prove, but the clarity made her wince, so this was not the day.

The third day she never knew the weather. She took a room in the motel. She checked in the night before to give herself plenty of time to think and perhaps even fall asleep if she got tired and wake up refreshed and ready to put in another day or week or month. She didn't fall asleep. She was wary and wakeful, watching the dullness of the pink and orange forms, the thick-waisted lampshade, the corner of the bed frozen in place like a colorized photograph of Niagara Falls.

She tried to think of the boys in the old, good days but was tortured by an image of the Betraying Husband squatting like a cheap statue on the bedside table.

She thought of the little girl she mentored on Saturdays, took shopping for lunch, to performances. But what good is the ballet, she thought, when the girl's mother keeps her out of school to clean house, and the stepfather feels up her new breasts? That child has no more chance than Stephen's quick broken neck in the car accident or James' inexorable bipolar disorder.

James said, I'm doing fine, Mom, much better! And bought the gun and rented the motel room. This motel, but not this room. At the other end. All her letters and petitions had not even made them hesitate when she purchased her weapon or when she rented the room.

She knew it was morning when light seeped under the drapes, washing out the perfect ugly colors. It didn't matter what kind of day it was. She had only wanted to prove how easy it was to rent the room, to purchase the firearm. She was too angry that day. She left the key in the motel office and went home.

December rain began as an ice storm, then changed over. She called in to work sick because she woke so heavy. She thought that this was the day. She would not have to be here for the holidays. She felt no relief, but a fittingness.

On the phone, their piping voices called: "Are you okay? You sound stopped up. You take it easy. Good-bye," they said.

She sat by the phone until the floating embers of human voices burnt out. This was where she had been alive for the past months, in the faint crackling of energy between the ones who called her and her hollow self. To make sure nothing else ignited, she unplugged the phone.

She examined what was left: a few objects in pouches and pockets. A silver charm, a pink lozenge of glass dropped hot on a surface and hardened with a flat bottom. A book she once read, a ticket for a museum exhibit, a perfect acorn with its little cap. Things that had given her a sense of riches, back when she used to dive into the green world.

She gathered up the babies in her arms, and they began to wiggle, and she said, Sleep, sleep, but the wiggle turned to struggle. Her arms weakened, her hands became clumsy. They escaped, grew large, broke apart. She could not save even one. It was not that her good things were worthless, and not even that they had lost their savor. They were as real as her suffering, but too few and too rare.

So, in the kitchen, with a black linoleum floor and black-out paint on the windows and the refrigerator carved of stone, and one small lightbulb casting just enough gray and feeble light to find the pistol in the drawer.

She didn't wait for the exact anniversary or the second reservation at the motel where her last son checked out.

Does not wait. Does not care for symmetry or statement or the effect on friends. She sits in the chair facing the wall and braces her elbows on the counter. She puts this bitter barrel in her mouth. She has practiced, in order to make no mistakes. She scatters her memories.

All the jewels and charms of her life roll across the floor.

LAUREN YAFFE

OUTLINING YOUR NOVEL

Lauren Yaffe
Outlining Your Novel

WORKSHOP DESCRIPTION

Children generally thrive in a structured environment. The same is true for our literary "babies." Outlining your novel (or play/screenplay) will help identify structural problems early on—before you're 200 pages into your draft—and will greatly ease the writing of that draft. During this class we'll be outlining, summarizing, even writing scenes, so bring an idea for a novel and come prepared to write. Level: Intermediate to Advanced.

INSTRUCTOR BIOGRAPHY

Lauren Yaffe holds an MFA from Warren Wilson College. Her stories and poems have appeared in such journals as *Alaska Quarterly Review, Calliope, Cottonwood, Frigate, Mediphors* and *Word*; and her essays appear in the recently published anthology, *Voices from the Spectrum*, and the forthcoming anthology, *The Elephant in the Playroom*. She is currently working on a screenplay and series of children's books about worms, gardening and the environment.

LARA ZEISES

WRITING FOR ADOLESCENTS: FROM CONCEPTS TO CONTRACTS

SUPPLEMENTARY MATERIALS:

HANDOUTS: TIPS TO HELP YOU TAKE THE PLUNGE SOME
EXERCISES TO TRY

10 STEPS TO CRACKING THE YA MARKET

RESOURCES FOR ASPIRING YOUNG ADULT
AUTHORS

LARA'S BOOKSHELF:
21 CONTEMPORARY YA NOVELS EVERYONE
SHOULD READ BEFORE THE AGE OF 21

Lara Zeises
Writing For Adolescents: From Concepts To Contracts

WORKSHOP DESCRIPTION

This workshop will focus on what makes a great middle grade or young adult novel (character, voice, tone); different approaches to writing and revising the adolescent novel; current market trends (high concept vs. literary); and what steps you'll need to take to write (and sell!) that first book.

INSTRUCTOR BIOGRAPHY

Lara M. Zeises is the author of three novels for young adults. Her first, *Bringing Up the Bones* (2002), was named an honor book for the 2001 Delacorte Press Prize Competition. Her second, *Contents Under Pressure* (2004), began as her thesis project at Emerson College, where in 2001 she earned her MFA in creative writing. It has been named to the 2006 International Reading Association's Young Adult Choices list (among others) and was voted the 2006 Delaware Blue Hen Teen Book Award winner. Lara's third novel, *Anyone But You* (2005), was a *Teen People* Top 10 Pick. An excerpt from that project helped earn Lara a 2005 Emerging Artist Fellowship in Literature-Fiction from the Delaware Division of the Arts.

In addition to writing, Lara teaches part-time at the University of Delaware, where she received her BA in English-Journalism. She also facilitates creative writing workshops for both teens and adults. You can learn more about Laura and her work at *www.zeisgeist.com.*

Tips to Help You Take the Plunge
By Lara M. Zeises
www.zeisgeist.com

1. **Play the "what if?" game.** Every story starts with a seedling of something—a character, a setting, an idea of a theme. Instead of trying to force the seedling into a full-grown plant, give it time to germinate. Author David Lubar starts each writing day by opening a file and typing at least one "what if?" scenario. When he's looking for his next project, he reads through the list to see if there's anything there he can use. Entire NOVELS have sprouted from the seeds he plants in this daily exercise.

2. **Get to know your characters**. There are many ways to get in touch with your characters. Some people like to fill out character questionnaires; others prefer to write diary entries in a character's voice, or draft letters from one character to another. Of course, you often won't know everything about your character when you start to write his or her story. That's okay. In fact, if you did know everything about your character, there'd be no reason to tell their story, because then there's nothing left to discover!

3. **Learn to be comfortable with the not knowing**. Part of the beauty in plunging is that you *don't* know what happens next. People who subscribe to this method of writing often say they feel like their characters will lead them where they want to go, instead of the other way around. Others describe the writing as trance-like, saying they feel like they're just channeling a story that's coming from somewhere outside of themselves. The nature of plunging forces you to have faith in the process, and asks you to surrender the notion that you can control the story. By giving yourself over to the mystery, you're opening doors to your story that might otherwise stay locked.

4. **Take notes along the way**. Most writers who use detailed outlines do so because it helps them keep track of characters, plot points, and theme. Plungers don't have this kind of road map. It helps, then, to keep a file or scrap pad nearby where you can jot notes to yourself about threads you'd like to pick up later on, or character traits that need more development. Think of it as your trail of breadcrumbs, the ones that will help keep you from getting completely lost in the forest.

5. **Know when to reel it back in**. At some point, most plungers will feel their story spiraling out of control. There are two ways to deal with this. One, let it keep spiraling and know that you can tame the beast during the revision process. Or two, assess the need for some sort of outline. Yeah, that's right. I said *outline*. When coaching the students in my freshman comp classes, I often advise them to make "after-the-fact" outlines. This is for when they get stuck on a first draft, or have a draft sorely in need of structure. I tell them to make a map of what they've got so that they can see gaps in logical development, or places where they haven't fully explained something or adequately set up a concept. This kind of outline can work for fiction as well.

Some Exercises to Try
By Lara M. Zeises
www.zeisgeist.com

MURDER YOUR DARLINGS

Be brutal as you edit your own work—but only after you've written a complete draft.

Go through your manuscript and write in the margin how each scene/sequence in your draft pushes the story forward or reveals something new about your characters. Great scenes accomplish both, but if you find a scene that accomplishes neither, you either need to rewrite it or cut it all together.

STRUCTURING EXERCISE

Playing with a novel's structure can be a daunting task. The next time you get stuck, try this exercise.

1. Buy a pack of 3" x 5" index cards.
2. Chart your novel, recording each individual scene or sequence on one card at a time.
3. Lay your cards out on a large flat space to get a visual representation of your structure.
4. Now you can experiment with moving scenes or sequences by using the cards, instead of chopping up a Word document. When you are satisfied with the restructuring, you can go back into the novel or outline and make the changes to see how they fit.
5. This is also a good tool to use if you need help in identifying holes in plot or character development. Make notes on the cards where you need to add more information or details.

COLOR CODING YOUR MANUSCRIPT

This exercise focuses on helping you "diagnose" issues common with first drafts.

1. Print out a copy of your manuscript OR open the Word file and do a "save as" so that you have a copy you can safely mark up.
2. Create a color key that matches each color to whatever you're trying to chart. For example, you might want to see if different threads in the novel are carrying equal weight. Or you might want to check the balance between interior thought, dialogue, and action. Whatever criteria you decide on, assign each item its own color.
3. Now highlight the manuscript according to the colors you've chosen. This will give you another visual representation of how your novel is unfolding.

10 Steps to Cracking the YA Market
By Lara M. Zeises
www.zeisgeist.com

1. **Read, read, read—and read some more**. The boundaries of young adult writing are shifting constantly. To stay apprised, it's important to familiarize yourself with both the current and classic literature.

2. **Write a book that has a beginning, middle, and end**. This sounds like a no-brainer, but the truth is, many aspiring authors get so caught up in the *idea* of being an author, they forget to actually *be* one.

3. **Find a good critique group**. If you're not already part of a critique group, you should think about joining or forming one. Through organizations like SCBWI you can find groups open to new members, or members who want to exchange manuscripts one-on-one.

4. **Learn to love—or at least tolerate—revision**. Finding the perfect critique group isn't going to do much good if you're not open to the process of revision. No one—and I mean NO ONE—is above editing

5. **Get online**. Listservs—like those found on YahooGroups.com—can be a great resource for writers. You can also use the Internet to check out authors' websites, read book reviews, and learn more about the field in general. Membership to SCBWI grants you access to their home page, where you can download the most up-to-date information about conferences and other events.

6. **Put on your party face**. There isn't a single writer—or successful businessperson from *any* field—who can't attest to the power of networking. Challenge yourself to talk to as many people as possible, even if it's just to say hello and exchange business cards. (And NEVER leave your house without your business cards, because you never know when you might need them.)

7. **Create a battle plan**. When you're ready to send out your manuscript, start by making a comprehensive list of all of the editors and agents you want to target. Remember all those books you've been reading? Look at the ones that would share an audience with your book, find out who edited them, and add those editors to your list.

8. **Write a killer query letter**. Queries are your one-page chance to sell an editor or agent on two things: your manuscript and *you*. One book that helped me through the query-writing stage was *Your Novel Proposal: From Creation to Contract* by Blythe Camenson and Marshall J. Cook. The Writer's Market guides are another good resource.

9. **Keep writing**. Say one of the editors you've queried has asked to see a full draft of your manuscript. It can take up to three months (or longer!) to get a response from them. Do not—and I repeat, DO NOT—spend the time obsessively checking your e-mail and snail mailboxes. Instead, dive into a new project.

10. **Don't give up**. No matter where you are in terms of the publishing game—whether you're still writing the first draft of your first novel, or sending out a polished draft of your third novel for the second year running—don't give up. If being a YA author is truly your dream, you *will* make it happen. After all, it's not easy cracking the market, but it can be done.

Resources for Aspiring Young Adult Authors
by Lara M. Zeises
www.zeisgeist.com

(NOTE: This list is by no means exhaustive—it's just a sampling of some of the resources I and other writers I know have found particularly helpful.)

Non-Fiction Books

Aronson, Marc. *Exploding the Myths: The Truth about Teens and Reading.* Lanham, MD, Scarecrow Press: 2001.

Camenson, Blythe and Marshall J. Cook. *Your Novel Proposal: From Creation to Contract.* Cincinnati, OH, Writer's Digest Books: 1999.

Cart, Michael. *From Romance to Realism: 50 Years of Growth and Change in Young Adult Literature.* New York, Harper Collins: 1996.

Lamott, Anne. *Bird by Bird: Some Instructions on Writing and Life.* New York, Pantheon: 1994.

Periodicals

Booklist—http://www.ala.org/ala/booklist/booklist.htm
Children's Book Insider—http://www.write4kids.com/aboutcbi.html
Horn Book—http://www.hbook.com/index.shtml'
Kirkus—http://www.kirkusreviews.com
Publisher's Weekly—http://publishersweekly.com/
School Library Journal—http://www.schoollibraryjournal.com
VOYA—http://www.voya.com/

Websites

Children's Literature Resources—http://www.cynthialeitichsmith.com
The Purple Crayon—http://www.underdown.org
Smart Writers—http://www.smartwriters.com
YahooGroups—http://www.yahoogroups.com

Organizations

ALAN (Assembly on Literature for Adolescents of NCTE)—http://www.alan-ya.org/
American Library Association—http://www.ala.org
Association of Authors' Representatives—http://www.aar-online.org/
The Author's Guild—http://www.authorsguild.org/
Children's Book Guild—http://www.cbcbooks.org/
Mystery Writer's of America—http://www.mysterywriters.org/
Romance Writers of America—http://www.rwanational.org/
Society of Children's Book Writers and Illustrators—http://www.scbwi.org

Lara's Bookshelf:
21 Contemporary YA Novels Everyone Should Read before the Age of 21

I am constantly revising this list (every time I've distributed it the choices have been different from the last). It is by no means comprehensive; in fact, YA advocates would be shocked to see some of my choices. Burger Wuss *instead of* Feed? *How could you leave off* The Outsiders *and* The Chocolate War? *I repeat: it's not comprehensive. If anything, it's a quirky mix of some of my favorites—a sampling of several different authors, styles, and subgenres. Hope you enjoy!*

1. Anderson, Laurie Halse. *Speak.*
2. Anderson, M. T. *Burger Wuss.*
3. Block, Francesca Lia. *Dangerous Angels.*
4. Chbosky, Stephen. *The Perks of Being a Wallflower.*
5. Crutcher, Chris. *Staying Fat for Sarah Byrnes.*
6. Cushman, Karen. *Catherine, Called Birdy.*
7. Dessen, Sarah. *This Lullaby.*
8. Flinn, Alex. *Breathing Underwater.*
9. Frank, E.R. *Life Is Funny.*
10. Hautman, Pete. *Sweetblood.*
11. Jenkins, A. M. *Damage.*
12. Johnson, Angela. *The First Part Last.*
13. Lubar, David. *Sleeping Freshmen Never Lie.*
14. Marchetta, Melina. *Saving Francesca.*
15. McCafferty, Megan. *Sloppy Firsts.*
16. Nelson, Blake. *Girl: A Novel.*
17. Spinelli, Jerry. *Stargirl.*
18. Thomas, Rob. *Rats Saw God.*
19. Witlinger, Ellen. *Hard Love.*
20. Wolff, Virginia Euwer. *Make Lemonade.*
21. Zindel, Paul. *The Pigman.*

SIMONE ZELITCH

DIALOGUE: BEYOND "HE SAID/SHE SAID"

Simone Zelitch
Dialogue: Beyond "He Said/She Said"

WORKSHOP DESCRIPTION

We all know that there is a difference between an overheard conversation and written dialogue. But what creates that distinction? How can the way your characters speak define who they are? How can the pauses create suspense, or opportunities for reflection and description? We will move beyond basic "he said/she said" tags that mark most dialogue, and explore ways that the space between the words is the most important part of all. Level: Beginner

INSTRUCTOR BIOGRAPHY

Simone Zelitch is the author of three novels, including *Louisa* (Putnam, 2000), which was the winner of the Goldberg Prize for Emerging Jewish Fiction. Her work has been featured on the NPR broadcast and new anthology, *Hannukah Lights*. She teaches at Community College of Philadelphia, where she coordinates the Certificate Program in Creative Writing.

TOM ZOELLNER

THE ART AND CRAFT OF INVESTIGATIVE JOURNALISM

Tom Zoellner
The Art and Craft of Investigative Journalism

WORKSHOP DESCRIPTION

This is how you find the news that would otherwise never come to light—the high cancer rates in a certain neighborhood, the fat expense accounts at the respected charity, or the racial profiling in a city's police department. You have a hot tip, or a just a strong suspicion, but how do you really nail the story? We'll tell you how in this seminar, in which you can also expect to learn how to use public records to create a person's background profile, tricks for getting inside access to large institutions, methods for building the trust and confidence of sources, ways of rendering complex issues in real English and using the techniques of a novelist to tell compelling nonfiction stories.

INSTRUCTOR BIOGRAPHY

Tom Zoellner is a contributing editor for *Men's Health* magazine. During a twelve-year career in newspapers, he worked as a reporter for *the San Francisco Chronicle, The Arizona Republic,* and *The Salt Lake Tribune* and won numerous awards for his investigative stories. He is the author of *The Heartless Stone: A Journey Through the World of Diamonds, Deceit and Desire* (St. Martin's Press), and co-author of *An Ordinary Man* (Viking), the autobiography of Paul Rusesabagina, whose actions during the 1994 Rwandan genocide were portrayed in the movie *Hotel Rwanda.* More info on the book is available at *www.theheartlessstone.com*